THE DRUNKARD

Tom Murphy

Also by Tom Murphy

A Whistle in the Dark

On the Outside (w. Noel O'Donoghue)

On the Inside

A Crucial Week in the Life of a Grocer's Assistant

Famine

The Morning after Optimism

The Sanctuary Lamp

The Blue Macushla

The Informer (from the novel by Liam O'Flaherty)

Conversations on a Homecoming

Bailegangaire

A Thief of a Christmas

Too Late for Logic

The Patriot Game

She Stoops to Folly (from *The Vicar of Wakefield* by Oliver Goldsmith)

The Gigli Concert

The Wake

The House

The Cherry Orchard (a version)

THE DRUNKARD

Tom Murphy

After *The Drunkard* by W.H. Smith & A Gentleman

Carysfort Press

A Carysfort Press Book

The Drunkard

by Tom Murphy

First published in Ireland in 2004 as a paperback original by Carysfort Press, 58 Woodfield, Scholarstown Road, Dublin 16, Ireland

Typeset by Carysfort Press
Cover design by Alan Bennis
Front cover photograph courtesy of Colm Hogan
Printed and bound by eprint Limited
35 Coolmine Industrial Estate, Blanchardstown,
Dublin 15, Ireland

Published with the support of the Title by Title Grant from the Arts Council.

for jane

The Drunkard by Tom Murphy was first produced at the Town Hall Theatre, Galway, on July 18, 2003, by b*spoke theatre company in association with Galway Arts Festival, with the following cast:

Sir Arden Rencelaw	Nick Dunning
Edward Kilcullen	Rory Keenan
Phelim McGinty	Stephen Brennan
Mother/Agnes Earley/Floozie 1	Pauline McLynn
Arabella/Floozie 2	Sarah-Jane
Drummey	
William Earley/Loafer 3	Jack Lynch
Widdy Spindle/Tavern Keeper/ Loafer 1/Bartender/Policeman 2	Dylan Tighe
Farmer/Loafer 2/Policeman 1	Rory Nolan
Alanna/Village Girl/Floozie 3	Sarah Brennan
Village Girl	Gemma Reeves
Director	Lynne Parker
Set & Costume Design	Monica Frawley
Lighting Design	Rupert Murray
Music arranged, composed, and performed by	Ellen Cranitch & Hélène Montague
Stage Manager	Aisling Mooney
Assistant Stage Manager	Gemma Reeves
Producers	Jane Brennan & Alison McKenna

Acknowledgements

The Drunkard by Tom Murphy, after the melodrama by W.H. Smith and A Gentleman, is also indebted to *Ten Nights in a Bar Room* by William W. Pratt and *Fifteen Years of a Drunkard's Life* by Douglas Jerrold; and for lines, freely used, from *'Let The Toast Pass'* by R.B. Sheridan in Scene Two Act Two. Songs: the lullaby, 'Child and Mother' is by H.A.J. Campbell and Eugene Field; 'O Kisses They are Plenty' (anonymous); 'Down Among the Dead Men' is by Dyer; 'Soft Music is Stealing' is by F. Pax.

Additional music:

Additional, original music for the premiere of Tom Murphy's *The Drunkard* was composed and performed live by Ellen Cranitch and Hélène Montague. It included some set pieces – the wedding scene, the tavern scenes and the final 'hymn'. Extensive underscoring was also used almost continuously – this was devised in response to the rhythm of language, and the actions and interactions of the characters.

Characters

Sir Arden Rencelaw
Edward Kilcullen
Phelim McGinty, a lawyer
Arabella
Mother
Agnes Earley
Tavern-Keeper
William Earley
Alanna, a child
Widdy Spindle
Bartender
Man
Villagers, Loafers, Floozies, Policemen

The play benefits from a musical accompaniment.

Prologue

The prologue is delivered by Sir Arden Rencelaw, *dramatist and philanthropist. He is innocently himself.*

Rencelaw: When steadfast man, with riches to enjoy, well-born and nobly to ambition's cause intent, begins to slide into perdition's way, what topples him? What insidious attraction tempts the tender heart from that straight and goodly narrow to the rude bent and vulgar broad? Why, when in safe harbour, his wont to drift the foul-hard foetid waters from the soft moorings of a lovely wife?

Apply to Intellect's highest school, man's overflowing treasury of light, philosophy, and draw a blank. And the Holy Alternative in His infinite wisdom guards His motives still. Our heavenward appeal is not for answer but to implore first aid.

Yet, I have some, and not a little knowledge of this turpi-tude, for I was once – though never wedded – one such.

Taxing to credit when you see before you a personage of my conduct. But 'tis shining reformation o'er my erstwhile fault that you perceive; a figure staunch again in the ways of righteousness, reconstituted in fortune and, though I am not one to boast, in just and rightful claim to fame. Indeed, in recognition of a life spent penning works for the edification of my fellow man, titled. Don'tcha know.

But that is perfunctory by the way, for the protagonist of the drama to be here enacted is not its humble author: the role I take is more modest one, God's instrument on earth.

Lights briefly up on a bundle of rags that is Edward, *lying in a heap on the ground.*

There he is, the hero, master of the earth and all its creatures. There he lies, man, who binds the elements to his will, at death's door, gorged to the throat with wine.

Is't too late for him to mend? Can the luminous, once-noble light, now guttering to its shivering last, have rekindle? Is't too late? Is't too late for YOU? Fellow, fallible man, I stand before you, renovation's living proof! All can be saved.

Light briefly up on McGinty *– his back towards us, perhaps.*

Most all. For there are some, into whose hearts, black and adamantine, no ray of sweetness is allowed to penetrate, who will continue blind to example's lamp and resolutely deaf to the reproving shafts of conscience. Why? In this request we are afforded no difficulty. For no reason other than that someone *pitied* them.

Take observation then and attend the tale of human weakness about to be revealed, of selfless and unfaltering love to rend and yet uplift the gentle heart; a tale of re-morseless hatred, cruel injustice and salvation. Poor woman.

The last, as he leaves, of Mother *who is entering scene one. Music.*

ACT ONE

Scene One

An idyllic, rural cottage. A chair ... Mother, *an apple-cheeked, old lady, has entered, leaning on a stick. She starts, totters, as if seeing a ghost.*

Arabella, *who will come hurrying in in a moment with a basket of flowers, is young, beautiful, spirited and very kind.*

Mother: Oooooo!

Arabella: Mother! Mother!

Mother: *(to her)* Bartholemew!

Arabella: Mother?

Mother: Your dear father – *(She points to a spot, whispers:)* Bartholemew.

Arabella: Shriek! *(Then:)* There is nothing there. Morning light through the lattice contrives in variegated hues to dissemble, amusingly.

Mother: No, my dear. It was on that spot your dear father breathed his last.

Arabella: Oh, Mother. Let me help you to the chair.

Mother: That chair is indeed dear to me.

Arabella: There. *(Seating her)*

Mother: For it was in this chair he sat the day before he passed away. Oh how he loved this calm retreat! And 'twas often in his last illness, he ... he –

Arabella: He rejoiced in you, mother.

Mother: He rejoiced in me, Arabella. The comfort he drew from the knowledge that it should be myself would close his eyes at last to these rural shades; ah yes, and soon follow him, to be laid in yon little nook abroad out there beside him. And what is more –

Arabella: Dearest, dearest, *dearest*, Mother, it is true that this cottage, and its contents, are most dear to us, but we are not the proprietors, and now word is abroad that our worthy landlord, Patrick Joseph Kilcullen, is failing fast.

Mother: Aa no! Old Paddy Joe?

Arabella: I fear so. And should he cease the world we would be left in the hands of his son, Young Edward Kilcullen, who has come down from college, word on whom is scant other than that he has been paying nocturnal calls on the village tavern of late.

Mother: My beloved child! Who will protect you when I am gone?

Arabella: Oh dear, I did not mean to alarm you.

Mother: Hark!

A knock at the door.

That must be someone. Come in!

Enter McGinty**.**

McGinty: Good Mrs Clancy – Remember me? – One of the McGinty family below? – Now Lawyer McGinty. I once ran bare-foot in this village and knew your husband Bartley well, indeed I did and he knew me – Indeed I did – Good morning!

Mother: Good morning, sir!

Arabella: Sir! *(Curtseys)*

McGinty: Mmmm, young lady!

Mother: Arabella, child, a chair.

McGinty: Won't sit. A sad calamity has befallen the village.

Mother: Not? Aa no!

McGinty: Paddy Joe. I have lost a client, may he rest in peace.

Mother: The lenient creature! Many a poor person, I feel, will have reason to mourn his passing.

McGinty: Indeed they will, how true! A good old skin, a grand old stick and we'll leave it at that. He placed great confidence in me towards the end and I am now sole trustee and executor of all he owned, except this cottage.

Mother: Which favour he bequeathed to us in his final testament!

McGinty: Aaa, no now. *('Not so fast')* Which favour was transferred by *deed*, to his son, sometime in the past.

Arabella: To Young Edward Kilcullen?

McGinty: To the young buck Ned.

Arabella: Sir, you are skilled in pleading causes and I perceive in you a worthy advocate who has –

McGinty: A heart for business and a head to feel for the unfortunate – yes! So why prolong a matter that perhaps another dreads: Do ye have the money to purchase this property?

Mother: This calm retreat!

McGinty: *(To himself)* They don't have it.

Arabella: The young gentleman wishes to sell it?!

McGinty: What else can he do?! It's all that he possesses. Cut off with a shilling in his father's will – I saw to it myself!

Mother: It's the streets for us then!

McGinty: *(To himself)* The streets!

Mother: Is my child to be exposed to the thousand temptations of life?!

McGinty: Bear up! Your daughter's young and roundly beautiful: avid public interest must await such usefulness.

Arabella: *(To herself)* What if the rumour of this young man's character be in mistake or a tarnish put about by idle tongues?

McGinty: What's the young fruit thinking?

Arabella: *(To herself)* And I, with safety, could approach him with petition?

McGinty: No!

Arabella: Sir?

McGinty: Let me plead your case.

Arabella: But some instinct tells me deep inside –

McGinty: The young man's gay! grows fond of the world, fond of – Not edifying for the ears of sweet innocence.

Arabella: But –

McGinty: He's giddy! Be advised, my dear: Do not approach him, nor let him see you – unless I find advantage in it. I shall go to him at once and, man to man, make trial on your behalf.

Mother: Oh Sir! –

Arabella: Kind Sir! –

Mother: Dear Sir! -

McGinty: Tut, tut! Think nothing of it, that's the sort of man I am. In the meantime, lest my best entreaties fail of course, be looking for a place before he moves in the matter. Now I must be off. May heaven look down on you with blessings, if it can. (*Exit)*

Mother: A comfort to have such a friend in the hour of trouble?

Arabella: Yes, Mother. He appears a very feeling man *(to herself)* but what if *he* be in mistake about Young Edward Kilcullen's character? Arabella Clancy, it's vainglorious of you to be setting conjecture against the opinion of a learned man! But my instinct, now awakened, grows obstinate to see him. Tck, Arabella Clancy! that is female curiosity aroused, for you have heard too the young man's not too badly landscaped. Yes, but what if I, *in concert* then with our lawyer friend, made proposal of our own? Dare I? Arabella, will you stop! I wont! Mother, how much have we put aside to purchase fuel for the winter?

Mother: It's all here in the box.

Arabella: And if that were offered to him? –

Mother: Thirty shillings –

Arabella: It would partially do for our rent arrears.

Mother: And when the young man finds we are disposed to fairly deal with him? Yes, go to him!

Arabella: Yes, I shall go to him! –

Mother: And he'll relent! -

Arabella: He'll relent! *(She is putting on her village bonnet, etc. To herself:)* And yet, I tremble with a sad foreboding.

Mother: Why, child, you turn pale!

Arabella: Dearest Mother, it is nothing. A severe task is imposed on us, but it must be done.

Mother: And he'll relent! And if he be one whit like his father, he'll have the manners of a gentleman and, however wild his conduct when at large among the loafers, he'll not insult an unprotected woman.

Arabella: You give me courage.

Mother: Hand me down my book.

Arabella *gets the Bible, kisses it for strength and gives it to her mother.*

Mother: Go forth, my child; go as the dove from the ark of old and return with the olive branch of peace.

Arabella: Should I fail?

Mother: Return to find consolation here in the bosom of your fond old widowed mother. But you shall not fail.

Scene Two

(Drop scene) A landscape.

McGinty *and* Arabella, *en route to see* Edward Kilcullen, *alternate, coming forward and retiring.*

McGinty: Well, that little scene of sympathy and concern with Bartholemew Clancy's widow and daughter went well. Now for this young milk-sop puppy Kilcullen.

Arabella: In a few moments I shall come face to face with this young man whose tarnished reputation now alarmingly enlarges in my brain. Oh courage, Arabella!

McGinty: I now control all the Kilcullen family ever owned except the cottage, which final clause, when I possess it, will clinch a life's ambition.

Arabella: I'm nearly there – Dare I go on? I must go on, suppliant to a dangerous reprobate for shelter beneath the roof where I was born.

McGinty: Why? Firstly, for the *kindness* I for years endured from Patrick-Joseph-Paddy-Joe Kilcullen and, secondly – secondly, it doesn't suit me to think about it now.

Arabella: Do my mother's cheery urgings, my own innocent expectations deceive in leading me to hope of a notorious dissipated collegian?

McGinty: Ha! There he is.

Arabella: Shriek! A gentleman approaches.

McGinty: Wish-washed and starry-eyed.

Arabella: His fear-inspiring countenance informs me it is he.

McGinty: I cooked the father, now to prepare easier fare, the son. *(Exit)*

Arabella: I am tongue-tied. I must pause a moment for valour to recover. *(She retires)*

Enter Edward, *another innocent; young, handsome, earnest, somewhat dreamy and romantic.*

Edward: For the very sacred life of me I know not what to say to you – *(To heaven:)* Papa? The situation bears no comprehension. All these acres should be mine. What offence to merit disinheritance? That I enjoy a little – tipple – now and then? Hardly. Or that he thought I lacked – 'drive' – that my bashfulness was – 'unmanly'? I must say I am a trifle upset. *(To heaven:)* And what now up there, Papa, has Mama got to say to you in heaven, what does *she* think of you? 'Out and out with you, Paddy Joe!' she is saying, I'll wager. 'Out and out with you to treat your son – your *only* son – our only child like that!' *(He produces a hip-flask)* She at least left me a little something in cash. But that will hardly keep whatever-the-animal-is from the stable door when the fox has run off with all the chickens, will it? Hah! Out and out with you, Paddy Joe! *(And he has a sip from the flask)*

McGinty: *(Without)* Holloo! Young Master Kilcullen, Sir! *(Entering)*

Arabella: *(from afar)* Lawyer McGinty goes earnestly to plead our case.

McGinty: I bring good news!

Edward: You have found another will!

McGinty: What strange idea! Why, that thought has been so banished from my mind, there cannot be other than the one that cut you off. I conducted all your late dear father's business.

Edward: It don't make sense! Adoringly he looked me at the last – He drew me close. My very image was reflected in his eye – as I stand here I saw it there – an apple! Before heaven's very threshold he turned back and said, 'Forget the poetry, put your knuckles on the grindstone, and ever keep a special eye on those that heaven chose to bless less well than you, the tenantry'. Where is explanation? What tenantry?! for me to keep a special eye on.

McGinty: Your father was a saint sure. Who, but I, has reason never to forget the superiority of his existence? But like many a saint before him, he rambled at the last.

Edward: But father was so *wise* – Paddy Joe! The man could not even – *blink* – without there being something in his eye. What could he have in mind for me that is so encoded in his dying scripture? *(He is throwing his hands up)* I am bereft!

McGinty: But, Young Sir, you have the cottage, previously inherited by deed, which is the matter I have come about. I have opportunity of selling it.

Edward: Lost! *(He's not listening; sighs and has a sip)*

McGinty: For – A hundred pounds?

Edward: *(absently)* Did I not hear that it is occupied?

McGinty: By an impecunious old widow and her child.

Edward: Who have lived there long.

McGinty: In arrears for rent.

Edward: And that the widow is in poor health.

McGinty: She has a claim upon the poorhouse.

Edward: Hmm? *(He continues dreamily)*

McGinty: I have the eviction papers here, ready to be signed.

Edward: *(Then, suddenly)* I have tenants! Maybe I have little else but I have tenants to keep a special eye on! Do I at last begin to decipher some of father's philosophy?

McGinty: Young man –

Edward: Hold! Though I am now myself in somewhat straitened circumstances, that condition shall not make me less gentlemanly. Deprive peasant simplicity of a caring landlord! Of a home dear to them as a, perhaps a – popsy! Send them forth from the flowers they have cultivated, the vines they have trained in courses –

McGinty: No vines – *('Hot air')*

Edward: From an abode endeared to them by tenderest recollection and domestic remembrances of things past and gone.

McGinty: Oh! all that and more. The fences they've neglected, garden gate off its hinges, limbs of birch and fruit trees broken down for firewood – a window decorated with a battered hat!

Edward: Cease, McGinty! All this was explained to me by Billy Earley in the tavern last evening. The trees were broken down by idle schoolboys, and with regard to the battered hat in the window, whose hat was that, Sir? I ask you! It was a *man's* hat, Sir, the hat of Bartholemew Clancy, Sir! Can as much be said of yours, McGinty?

McGinty: I see you are pleased to be pleasant this morning and I bid you good day! *(He walks away, stops. To himself:)* This does not turn out.

Arabella: *(from afar)* He has argued well our case but his sombre face tells not of victory.

McGinty: I'll play my next advantage.

Arabella: He tries for us again – Courage to the lawyer!

McGinty: Beg pardon, Master Kilcullen, I now comprehend what underlies your plan the better. Let them stay on in the cottage for a term. The daughter, growing girl, eh? Tender, rosy, firm?

Edward*'s lack of comprehension.*

Aa, you have not seen her!

Edward: Never.

McGinty: Aaaaa!

Edward: Explain yourself.

McGinty: Continue them in residence till you're – Satisfied? Traps for wild fowl? Mother, daughter grateful – free access to the cottage at all hours – love, passion?

Edward: Do you know the girl has no father?

McGinty: That's it!

Edward: Are you aware that she is brotherless?

McGinty: A garden without a fence! All you have to do is step inside it.

Edward: That is – McGinty! – Shocking! To enter like a wolf an innocent fold and lie down with a lamb! Shocking! Tear from a mother's arms the last hope of her old age! If I had a horsewhip I would seize you by the throat and dash you prostrate to the earth! *(He moves away)*

McGinty: He's drunk!

Edward: *(Loudly)* Unmolested, the widow and her child shall remain in the cottage – Forever!

Arabella: Heavens! *(And she approaches)*

McGinty: Hell!

Edward: This is the widow's – *child*?

McGinty: And she is a dear girl. But I am deeply upset that a member of the family I have esteemed my lifelong years should so misconstrue my words.

Arabella: *(to* McGinty*)* Oh thank you, Sir! And blessings – blessings! – shower on you, Sir! *(She kneels at* Edward's *feet)*

Edward: She – she weeps?

McGinty: As I do. Deeply upset. *(As he exits)* I'll be revenged on them both for this.

Edward: By – by my soul!

Arabella: *(Weeping; to herself)* This is unexpected kindness, Arabella.

Edward: The lovely girl excites my sympathy, strangely. No! r-r-rise, M-m-miss.

Arabella: Clancy. I have an errand, Sir, for you.

Edward: What's this?

Arabella: 'Tis portion of the rent money we owe. Oh, but be assured of the remainder as soon as willing hands can earn it.

He stays her with a gesture.

But you declared that mother and I should remain in the cottage!

Edward: And I s-s-spoke it plain.

Arabella: What reason then to hold from you your due? – Take it!

Edward: N-n-nay!

Arabella: Take it, I entreat! Especially now you are in need of it. *(Hand to her mouth: was her last presumptuous?)*

Edward: *(is not offended; he is mustering himself against his shyness. Loudly)* Perish the rent money, Miss Clancy!

Arabella: What do I do with it?

Edward: Keep it!

Arabella: Ay?!

Edward: As portion of your dowry.

Arabella: Sir?

Edward: Shall I undisguise my feelings? Shall I?

Arabella: 'Twould be impertinent of me to order you in aught.

Edward: In plenitude are there comely maidens with beauty to astonish in this section of the country. But I have now discovered something more: a purity of mental excellence, noble sentiment and filial piety. These qualities my mother had, these were the charms that bound captive my father's heart and made man of him. I too would be such success as he. *(He throws the flask away behind his back)* I speak plainly for I speak honestly, and when I ask that you keep the contents of that box as portion of your dowry, need I say into whose hands I should like to have it fall at last?

Arabella: Shriek! But to affect not to understand you further, Sir, would be idle return for your kindness and condescension.

Edward: M-m-miss Clancy –

Arabella: Arabella.

Edward: I sometimes stroll in the vicinity of your cottage.

Arabella: Should I, M-m-mr Kilcullen –

Edward: Edward -

Arabella: See you go by without stopping, why then, why then –

Edward: Why then, why then, Miss Clancy?

Arabella: Why then – Oh Mr Kilcullen, I should suppose that you'd forgotten where I lived!

Edward: Yes, my father's wisdom worked in ways mysterious. A cottage, gifted to me by this deed on the day that I was born: that it should become a casket for a priceless jewel! Miss Clancy, in earnest of my trust, would you consent to have your name lie with mine on this document?

Arabella: Edward!

Edward: Arabella!

Music.

They exit.

In the transition, McGinty *returns and looks off in the direction they have taken.*

McGinty: Thus ends my efforts? *(He sees the discarded hip-flask and he picks it up)* Thus ends my efforts, for now.

He exits.

Scene Three

A platform on the village green for a celebration. Villagers in festive spirit enter for the party: William Earley, Girls *(including an oddly-dressed* Widdy Spindle*),* Farmer *and* McGinty *too, affecting goodwill. They are led in by* Rencelaw*, who is in peasant dress – his 'disguise' – a pied piper with a tin whistle. (The men have tankards of drink)*

All: Ha, ha, ha, ha, ha, ha, ha!

Rencelaw: The village keeps holiday for the newly-weds!

All: Ha, ha, ha, ha, ha, ha, ha!

Rencelaw: *(Calling off)* Stay you a while there, the rest of you! You shall all have chance to show your mettle!

McGinty: Ha, ha, ha! – Great happiness attends us all!

All: Ha, ha, ha, ha, ha!

Rencelaw: Yes, warm the village green with honest, wholesome merriment for the arrival of the happy couple! Select partners!

William: Widdy Spindle, let's see what's left in them relic pins! *(Dances with her)*

Spindle: William Earley, how uncouthful!

All dancing

Rencelaw: Vary partners!

All dancing, they change partners.

Rencelaw: Single dancers!

Others: Widdy Spindle, take the floor! Widdy Spindle! *(Etc.)*

Spindle: Nay! 'tis too much for my temerity!

And she leaps into the dance, the others cheering on her solo performance.

Farmer: Now for William's turn!

Others: William! Billy! (*Etc.*)

William: *(dancing solo:)*

When I was a young and roving boy,
Where fancy led me I did wander;
Sweet Caroline was my pride and joy,
But I missed the goose and hit the gander.

Clapping, cheering – 'Next!' 'Who's next?' – *and* Rencelaw *takes the floor:*

Rencelaw: Well-executed, honest William, but – Everybody! – observe how I do it!

When I was a young and roving boy,
Where fancy led that road I'd take;
Sweet Angeline was my pride and joy,
But I missed the goose and hit the drake.

Laughter, applause etc.

Spindle: Who is he? Who is that handsome, vigorous *(*young*)* man?

Rencelaw: *(Aside)* When visiting the provinces, I sometimes conceal myself lest my fame put them in awe.

Farmer: That be Sir Arden Rencelaw in his disguise.

William: Likes to be up and down the country –

Farmer: A-couragin' what be right, a-curin' what be wrong.

Girls: A ring-play, a ring-play!

Rencelaw: Form a circle! –

William: Fall in here! –

Girls: A ring-play, a ring-play! –

McGinty: Sweet golden age of youth! –

Spindle: Who'll go in the middle? –

McGinty: Aa, that I were young again! –

William: Lawyer McGinty!

McGinty *protesting*

All: Honest Lawyer McGinty!

He is pushed into the centre –

William: There's a right, rich catch for you, ladies! –

And they circle him –

Girls: I am a rich widow, I live all alone;
I have but one son and he is my own.
Go, son – go, son – go choose you one –
Go choose a good one or else choose none!

All: Choose! Choose! … *(Laughter)*

Improvise. McGinty *succumbs to a shy, giggling side of his nature – whatever – as* Girls *are pushed at him or he grabs at the* Girls *…* Spindle *finds herself with* McGinty.

Men: Kiss her, McGinty!

Spindle: Mortifications!

Girls: Kiss him, Widdy Spindle!

Spindle: Petrafactions!

Farcical kiss. Cheers. And McGinty *and* Spindle *dance, while:*

All: *(circle them:)*

Now you are married, you must obey
What you have heard your parents say;
Now you are married, you must prove true –
As you see others do, so do you!

William: Mary and Joseph!

He's impatient at this 'clumsy' dance, he sweeps Spindle *from* McGinty *and they dance together, vigorously:*

Mercy on me! What have you done?
You married the father instead of the son!
His legs are crooked and ill put on.
They're all laughing, Widdy Spindle, at your young man.

Laughter, cheering. Then a gradual hush and they pull back as Agnes *comes in, singing to herself, smiling, laughing crazily, and strewing a few withered flowers.*

Agnes: *(without)*

Brake and fern and cypress dell
Where slippery adder crawls …

McGinty: The maniac, Agnes Earley. Her voice haunts me like the spectre of that young shuffler she was to marry.

Agnes: Brake and fern and cypress dell
Where slippery adder crawls,
Where grassy waters well
By the old moss-covered walls ...

(To various people, in turn:) Will you come to my wedding today and see the coffin go in? Will you come to my wedding today and ... *(Etc)*

Spindle: *(to* Rencelaw*)* She were to be married, Sir, but night afore wedding her young man up and died –

Girl: Outside the tavern.

Spindle: Fell-n-died in a drunken fit.

Farmer: Aye!

McGinty: Her eyes! Maniacs have strange insight. She knows too much for my happiness.

Agnes: *(To* McGinty*)* Will you come to my wedding today–

McGinty: Go home, Agnes, you creature! –

Agnes: And see the coffin go in?

McGinty: Who let her out?! Why is she here?! –

Agnes: And we shall dance! *(She dances gaily)*

Upon the heather, when the weather
Is as mild as May,
So they prance as they dance
And we'll all be happy and ...

(It's dying on her) And we'll all be happy and ... *(She cries:)* Water! Water! He only wanted water! ... Water ... But they kept feeding red ... *red-red-red* water ... into poor young Kevin's glass.

Rencelaw: Ah, *red* water!

Agnes: Quick! – Give him water – Quick! Oh hear him cry for water! Quick, quick! he turns cold. Quick! his lips, the lips I love ... turn blue ...*(To* McGinty*)* Sir?

McGinty: Why can't the Almshouse keep these maniacs chained up?! It's a disgrace! She should not be at large! Look at her!

Agnes: *(Laughs/sing-songs?)* The lawyer is a creepy man, now owns the brick house yonder!

McGinty: She ruins our honest celebrations, she distresses the entire neighbourhood! – the poor wretch! Agnes, you *witch*, clear off from here!

Agnes: And the will – Ha, ha, ha!

McGinty: Wha's'at?! –

Agnes: The will – Ha, ha, ha!

McGinty: So, you want a nice warm whipping? – *(He fetches a cane)*

Agnes: The will – Ha, ha, ha!

McGinty: Then you shall have one!

His cane is raised to strike Agnes*, who is now cowering on the floor.* Rencelaw, *with deft flick of his own cane, knocks the cane out of* McGinty*'s hand; and* William, *too, has rushed in to throw* McGinty *aside.*

Rencelaw: Fie!

William: Ho! Strike my helpless, little, half-crazed sister Agnes, would you?!

McGinty: Assault and battery! All here are witnesses!

William: Ho! Ho! Mr Honey! – I wont wait for Bezzelybub down there –

McGinty: I'll have you, William Earley, between stone walls! –

William: To treat you to a brimstone bath! –

Rencelaw: Silence! ... I have some, and not a little, knowledge of physic and I suspect this young lady's malady to be temporary ... Miss Agnes?

Agnes: Sir? will you come to my wedding today ...and marry me? *(In tears)*

Rencelaw: I should be greatly honoured.

Agnes: Then walk up, young man, there's a lady here, with ... *(she cowers again)*

Rencelaw: With jewels in her hair. *(He has approached her and is holding out his hand to her)*

She considers his hand, hesitates, withdraws into herself, and retreats from them –

Agnes: 'Brake and fern and cypress dell where slippery adder crawls ...'

And she is gone. Rencelaw, *interested, follows her a little way. The dancing has started again. And this turns into a guard-of-honour for the arrival of the bride and groom,* Arabella *and* Edward, *accompanied by* Mother. *Church bells, rose petals, cheering.*

Hooray! Hooray!
Hail, hail, the happy pair!
Long life!
Peace! Health and joy!
Progeny!

Happiness!
Hooray! Hooray!

The girls surround Arabella *to kiss her and admire her ring. And* Arabella *throws her bouquet of flowers up among them. While the* Men, *with their tankards, surround* Edward, *to shake his hand and toast him.* Edward *is a happy groom; shy, too, and nervous.*

McGinty: Toast to the groom!

Farmer: Aye: –

William: Aye, toast to the groom! –

McGinty: Your health, Master Edward!

William: Long life, Ned, and –

First Farmer: Aye! -

William: May the Kilcullen name be perpetuated!

McGinty: *(As they are about to drink)* Why, he has no cup! *(And he sends* Tom, *the* Farmer, *off to get one)*

Edward: Nay, Tom, thank you, but! *(Too late)*

McGinty: Nay? And offend by not returning the traditional toast?

Edward: My thanks, good friends all, but I have given up the practice and left the brawl of the tavern for a new beginning; and from today I am an altered man. *(And an aside to* Farmer *who has returned with a tankard of drink for him)* Nay, Tom.

McGinty: Excellent! An altared man – he's been to the altar – A wit, a wit! – he's jesting! *(Laughter)*

Edward: *(Laughing, nervously)* Nay –

William: Ah, here's to the bashful groom then!

McGinty: *(Holding up the toast)* Bashful?! Bashful?! His dear father once told me his bashfulness was such that he went to bed without a candle. *(Laughter)* What is to happen at bedtime tonight? *(Laughter)*

Edward: *(Takes the tankard)* Well, *one* draught then. For medicinal reasons. And – dearest and best of good fellows – so as not to be discourteous to your salute, this to *your* good health!

They drink. McGinty *draws Edward aside, produces the hip-flask and slips it to* Edward. Edward *is unsure.*

McGinty: As a precaution for later, lest your courage fail and take from the pleasure that lies ahead.

Mother: My children! This is a day of great joy. May blessings rest on you always. *(She joins the hands of* Arabella *and* Edward*)* And blessings be upon us all!

Applause.

Edward: From tomorrow all happiness shall be ours.

Arabella: Tomorrow? Why from tomorrow?

Edward: It will be the first full day of our union. *(He slips the flask into his pocket)*

Arabella: My husband.

Edward: My wife.

Music. They kiss. And they waltz off.

Scene Four

Arabella *sits alone by a cradle.*

Rencelaw: Tempus fugit. No longer does she address herself as Arabella Clancy, no longer the charming little cries of innocent astonishment that marked her girlhood. She is now wife and mother ... See her. She sleeps? Ah, no! She waits, hopes. She listens, ears pricking up like terriers for the rattle of the latch, the bride of only yesteryear shorn of glorious bloom. Or for the thunder of drunken fists upon the door that will alarm the ancient mother, now failing fast; that will awaken the newborn babe from sleep. She sings.

Arabella:

> Oh, Daughter-my-love, if you'll give me your hand
> And go where I ask you to wander,
> I will lead us away to a beautiful land –
> The Dreamland that's waiting out yonder;
> We'll walk in the sweet-posie garden out there,
> Where moonlight and starlight are streaming,
> And the flowers and the birds are filling the air
> With perfume and music of dreaming.

Rencelaw: Night after night she wastes the light of two candles. A hundred times has she crept to the casement, bending low her ear his step to catch. Many a despairing look has she cast at the black sky. Then moving back again, she pauses ...'Mother?'

Arabella: Mother? Are you all right?

Rencelaw: And returning to her child, she sits once more ... See her. She weeps? Ah, no! Stoically, she restrains her anguish ...'Edward?'

Arabella: Edward?

Rencelaw: Edward.

Edward: *(A light comes up on him)* I shall give it up. I promise.

Rencelaw: 'She is a good wife.'

Edward: And I worship her. And I shall reform.

Arabella: Kiss me?

Edward: I kiss you.

Rencelaw: 'Edward?'

Arabella: Edward?

Edward: I shall have one glass more.

Light down on Edward, *then down on* Rencelaw.

Arabella:

So, Daughter-my-love, let me take your dear hand
And away through the starlight we'll wander,
Away through the mists to the beautiful land –
The Dreamland that's waiting out yonder.

Scene Five

Exterior of the village tavern. A tree. Night.

Rencelaw: Half-a-dozen years elapse.

Noise and shouting in the tavern: Edward, *without his jacket, is being thrown out of the tavern – and is resisting it – by* Tavern-Keeper *(*Tubbs*); he goes back in again to be thrown out again.* McGinty *comes scurrying from the tavern – out of harm's way – to watch, pleased, from a distance.*

Farmer, *too, is here, paralytic; his monosyllabic contributions – 'Aye!' – are both belches and half-conscious responses to the drama going on about him.* William, *who has not been in the tavern, will arrive shortly.* Rencelaw *stands on the opposite side to* McGinty.

A sextet that grows: six voices in competition, in counter-part, over-lapping and simultaneous. (Improvise/ experiment)

Tavern-Keeper: Come along now –

Edward: I shall not leave –

Tavern-Keeper: *(Continuous/overlapping)* Come along, I say –

Edward: *(Continuous/overlapping)* How dare you, Sir –

Tavern-Keeper: Out of here –

Edward: I shall not leave –

Tavern-Keeper: Get out!

Edward: I shant!

Farmer: Aye!

Rencelaw: The business of his day is to get drunk!

McGinty: Life works admirably!

Tavern-Keeper: Come along now! –

Edward: I shall not leave! –

Tavern-Keeper: Come along I say! –

Edward: How dare you, Sir!

Tavern-Keeper: Out of here! – Get out!

Edward: I shall not leave! – I shant!

Farmer: Aye!

Rencelaw: The infatuation every day increases!

McGinty: Admirably! Admirably!

Tavern-Keeper: You'll have nothing more in this house tonight! –

Edward: Do you know whom you address?! –

Tavern-Keeper: Clear off! Clear off!

Farmer: Aye!

Rencelaw: He expels reason, drowns the memory, defaces beauty!

McGinty: Ha, ha, ha, ha!

William: Holloo! Holloo! What sport goes forward here? *(Arriving)*

Tavern-Keeper: Out, out-out! –

Edward: Release! – Unhand! –

Tavern-Keeper: Out, out-out! –

Edward: Release! – Unhand! –

Tavern-Keeper: Out, out-out, out-out!

Edward: Release! – Unhand me – Backslider!

Farmer: Aye!

Rencelaw: He thieves his pocket, devils his soul, diminishes his strength! –

McGinty: Ha, ha, ha, ha! Ha, ha, ha, ha!

William: Mary and Joseph, this ain't be no sport! –

Tavern-Keeper: Nothing more in this Christian house without money in his purse! –

Edward: I am a Kilcullen! –

Tavern-Keeper: Nor any other night for you!

William: Steady on! –

Edward: Dare you refuse service to a Kilcullen! –

Farmer: Aye!

Rencelaw: He drinks to others good health and robs himself of his own!

McGinty: Ha, ha, ha, ha! Ha, ha, ha, ha!

Edward: In this townland of Glencullen?! –

Tavern-Keeper: Nor-any-other-night!

William: Steady on! Edward, friend! Landlord Tubbs! –

Farmer: Aye!

Rencelaw: Bewitches his senses, corrupts his blood and causes internal and external injuries! –

McGinty: And he won't stop now – Ha, ha, ha!

Tavern-Keeper: Take 'His Lordship' out of this, William Earley!

Edward: If it were not for your greying hairs I'd thrash you within an inch of up-and-down the village! –

Farmer: Aye! –

William: Where's his coat then, Landlord Tubbs?

Tavern-Keeper: There's his coat then! *(Throws it on the ground)* Now, pack off! *(Exit)*

In the comparative quiet, Edward *is fuming, his anger and impotence making him pace/strut.*

Edward: This is an outrage, this is a scandal.

Farmer: Aye!

William: Come, Ned, let me advise you to go home.

Edward: *(Calling)* Tubbs! You in there! Don't want your flat, polluted, rot-gut liquor!

Tavern-Keeper: *(Off)* Ho, ho, ho, ho, ho!

Farmer: Aye!

William: Come, Ned –

Edward: Pack off! *(A shout at* Farmer*)*

William: Put on your coat -

Edward: *(At tavern)* Ho, ho, ho, ho, ho!

Farmer: *(exit)* Aye!

Edward: *(To himself)* But I know where liquor can be found.

William: Ned, friend, Ned! Your wife and child await.

Edward: And mother-in-law?

William: She's near the end, Edward, and suffering.

Edward: She is preparing for hell! *(In the next moment, horror: was that his voice; in the next moment, harshly:)* Ha, ha, ha, ha!

William: *(helping* Edward *into his coat)* You go more astray by the day than my little half-crazed sister Agnes. That's why I'm giving it up.

Edward: *('sincerity')* William, Billy, shipmate, brother! I need a moment alone to collect myself. You go on and, should you be passing, tell them that I shall be there, the briefest of anons, twinkling of a lamb's tail.

He watches William *go. Then he looks about:*

No one sees. Yes, I know where liquor can be found.

He goes to the tree and, from a hollow, produces a bottle.

McGinty: The arch cunning!

Rencelaw: Is this to be the issue of that young man's life?

Edward: *(Drinks)* Aaaaa! it relieves.

McGinty: He has tasted well and will not stop now – short of madness or oblivion.

Edward: *(drinks again, and)* Aaaaa! *(And sits under the tree to drink the rest)*

Rencelaw: Must he ever yield to the fell tempter and, bending like a bulrush to the blast, bow his manhood lower than the brute.

Edward: Aaaaa!

McGinty: I now know his nature well. I bide my time. *(Retires)*

Edward: *(To heaven: laughing to himself)* Papa – You up there – Dad! – whatchoo think of me now?

Rencelaw: And he could earn his bread.

Edward: If I wanted to.

Rencelaw: He has hands to work with, feet to walk, eyes to see.

Edward: *(Of his hands)* Merest of shakes.

Rencelaw: A brain to think.

Edward: Slight head *(Headache)*

Rencelaw: Yet these best gifts of heaven he abuses, and puts out the light of reason.

Edward: *(To the bottle)* Shapely friend, why do people so rail against you? *(And drinks)*

From afar in the night, eerily, faintly, plaintively:

Agnes: *(Off)* 'Brake and fern and cypress dell, where slippery adder crawls …'

Rencelaw: But another mission that brooks no wait calls upon my conscience and attention. *(He exits, purposefully)*

Edward: Poor Agnes, too, abroad the night again. *(To the empty bottle:)* And you, my friend, have nothing more to say to me. Can I now go home? Face them? *(Rises)* Mama, send down a little cash for Teddykins. *(Sighs)* If I had one more. From where?

McGinty: Master Edward, dear friend!

Edward: Tempter, begone!

McGinty: What means this?

Edward: Were you not with me in the tavern when that vile fray began?

McGinty: Fray? What fray?

Edward: And did you not desert me?

McGinty: But I was summoned out on urgent business!

Edward: *(Angrily)* Oh yes, oh yes, McGinty: you know only too well how to sit on the fence of the faraway hills buttering your bread on both sides where the grass is greener without batting a single blind eye when a friend is in trouble! Till the cows come home.

McGinty: But I left you jovial there! Remember, we two, 'Ha, ha, ha, ha!'? ... As I am a Christian!

Edward: Ha, ha, ha, ha! *(And throws his arms round* McGinty*:)* Tempter, begone! *(Then sighs)* Oh my friend, I am so ashamed and want for money.

McGinty: Want for? Pooh-Pooh! Do you see yon smoke, Sir, rising up among the trees?

Edward: Where?

McGinty: There.

Edward: Rising from – Cottage?

McGinty: Your cottage.

Edward: My cottage.

McGinty: And do you know how much it's worth, Sir?

Edward: How much, Sir?

McGinty: A full one hundred and fifty pounds, Sir.

Edward: A full ... *(And mouths the rest of it)*

McGinty: *(To himself)* I have him.

Edward: *(To himself)* Is he be pulling a trick down the sleeve of his mind? *(He points at* McGinty, *breaking away from him, laughing:)* Aaaaaa ...!

McGinty: The idiot's going to confuse it. Young Sir?

Edward: Do you know, do you know who had that cottage built, McGinty?

McGinty: Your father had that cottage built – Kilcullen.

Edward: My father had that cottage built, McGinty.

McGinty: And you came into it by the deed that's in your pocket on the day that you were born.

Edward: Is – that – so?! Well, can you tell me, then, by whom it was first occupied?! on the day that I was born.

McGinty: By a Mr Clancy.

Edward: By a Mr Clancy, McGinty.

McGinty: Bartholemew Clancy – Kilcullen.

Edward: Who?

McGinty: *(To himself)* This is stumbling search for cunning. Your point of argument, Sir.

Edward: Who lives there now?

McGinty: You do.

Edward: I do! I do!

McGinty: And your point!

Edward: Where do you live?

McGinty: Brick house yonder.

Edward: Brick house yonder, and see! – *(points)* – no smoke curlings. But see – there! – smoke rising up among yon trees?

McGinty: *(Exasperated)* And 'tis well established that you live there!

Edward: And no one else?

McGinty: Your family!

Edward: Beg pardon?

McGinty: Family!

Edward: ... Exactly! And you counsel me to sell it? Take a – a *nest* from a mourning bird and her – her *chick*! Make of them wandering – *scratchers* – of the world! And for what? I ask you! To put a little – *pelf* – into these leprous hands of mine – one hundred and fifty pounds, pah! – and to then squander it on – *Rum*?!

McGinty: *(To himself: 'I see')* I shall have to up the offer. But I must have that cottage.

Edward: And I must now go home.

McGinty: But not thus! You should first wash, refresh yourself.

Edward: Ought I?

McGinty: Yes!

Edward: Should I?

McGinty: Come with me.

Edward: Is it indeed for the best?

McGinty: Yes!

Edward: And not too late?

McGinty: No! And I have – *Rum*?

Edward: Brandy.

McGinty: A *feast* of it.

Edward: Well …But you are dry, McGinty, dull and steady: No man sits down with Teddy that don't drink glass for glass with him.

McGinty: Why, I can drink like an emperor.

Edward: Can you?

McGinty: *(Exiting)* This way! Come!

Edward: *(Solo)* We shall see who is last to finish first under the table.

He exits, following McGinty. *And* Agnes *enters, cautiously, to watch him go. Now she looks about, as* Edward *did earlier.*

Agnes: No one sees. *(And goes to the tree to draw from the hollow an imaginary bottle – or the empty one. She drinks from it, and:)* Aaaaaa! *(And again, and:)* Aaaaaa!

The moon is in and out of the clouds and shadows appear to move. Agnes, *a substantial fairy, dances in and out of the pools of light and talks to 'people'.*

Agnes: When we are married, will you come and visit? Do come! For we shall live but a little way away: Yes, in the valley, my dear. *(To another pool of light. She appears to be pouring tea)* This is special tea. For when I lived in the big house there was a blend that Mrs Kilcullen liked: not to my stomach. Yukky! And signs are on her now? The wings growing out of her back. No, taste this. Dock tea. What did I tell you? From your own back yard, made from the seeds of the dock.

She thinks she hears something, and she is poised to run if needs be. She forgets it.

We shall live down the valley
In a house all painted red –

Again, she thinks she hears something. And forgets it.

And every day the birds will come
To pick the crumbs of bread.

Indeed, she has heard something, because two crouched Figures, *using the shadows for cover, are entering stealthily … One* Figure *now is whispering:*

Figure: 'Hist! Do not make a sound …Be ready to spring if she tries to escape … Hist! Cut her off!'

The last because Agnes *is now darting this way and that, to escape. The* Figures *are* Rencelaw *and* William. *We establish who they are at whatever point. They have cut off* Agnes's *escape. She is frightened, but a kind of delighted terror, too, is growing in her. She begins to tremble, half-laughing, half-crying, half-defiant; indeed provocatively.*

Agnes: Kisses they are plenty as the blossoms on a tree!

Rencelaw: *(Whispering)* Miss Agnes ...Miss Agnes ... I am a friend to the unfortunate ... Hist! Cut her off!

Agnes: *(Has darted again; stopped)* Kisses they are plenty as the blossoms on a tree!

Rencelaw: We may yet need the net, William ... Miss Agnes, it is I, Sir Arden Rencelaw.

Agnes: *(Darts again, stops, and:)* Oh kisses they are plenty!

William: *(Tearfully?)* Oh Sir, be you sure that you know what you're doing with my sister?

They are closing in on Agnes*; all three, dipping, swaying, lunging: a kind of dance.*

Rencelaw: *(Singing quietly)* 'Oh kisses they are plenty' – I am taking her back to the big city, honest William, and putting her into care – 'Oh kisses they are plenty as the' – to have her malady treated. Don'tcha know. And you shall accompany us – Hist! Cut her off!

Agnes: *(Darted again, stopped again)* 'Kisses they are plenty as the blossoms on the tree!'

Rencelaw: And I suspect she is the key to much that is awry in these parts. Sing, William!

Rencelaw *and* William *sing the following as they close in on* Agnes*:*

Oh kisses they are plenty
as the blossoms on a tree.
And they be one and twenty
and are sweet to you and me;
And some are for the forehead,
and some are for the lips,
And some are for the rosy cheeks,
and some for fingertips;
And some are for the dimples,
but the sweetest one is this –

Agnes: 'When the bonny, bonny sweetheart gives his lady bride a kiss.'

During the above, Rencelaw, *magically – as only he can – has produced a net or a stream of long, coloured ribbons, which – with* William's *assistance? – is cast over/ draped upon* Agnes, *calming the trembling creature. She is tearful (?), smiles at them, and she walks off with them, her pages, like a bride.*

Music.

In the transition, Edward *and* McGinty *appear.* Edward *first, backing away from* McGinty, *pointing at him with the rolled-up document (deeds to the cottage), laughing:*

Edward: Aaaaaaaa …!

Both are drunk; McGinty, *indeed, who is following, is drunk to the point of being on his hands and knees, his hand reaching out to the document:*

McGinty: Let me touch it … Let me hold it … Let me feel it …

Edward: But look you! *(Unrolls document, shows it to* McGinty*)*

McGinty: I'll give you, I'll give you ... What did I last offer you?

Edward: But look! Two names on it, two signatures: My name and my wife's name.

McGinty: Nife's wame? Nife's wame?

Edward: You are, Maginty, killarneyed! Blind drunk! *(And exits)* 'I've been drinking, I've been drinking where were wine and brandy good ...'

McGinty: Nife's wame?... Wife's name! *(Thinks about it. And holds up his finger: he has the solution)* I'll have that cottage. I'll have everything the Kilcullens ever owned. Why? It suits me – *pleases* – to brood upon it now.

Old Patrick-Joseph-Paddy-Joe, ever a man for counting his possessions and his beads, tracked me one day, feather by feather, to a chicken I had plucked out of his yard. I was a boy of ten, and barefoot. He gave me personal pardon, soundly, with his whip, which I accepted and expected – which gratified me! For had he chosen to yield me to the authorities – minor though the offence – it would have meant imprisonment for someone of my station. But when he then informed me that he pitied me? In that moment I discovered myself. That he despised me thereafter is of no issue. From that moment I hated with an intensity – Ha, ha, ha! – that has existed beyond the grave, descending unimpaired to his expensively educated 'clever' son. By cunning – of which I have in plenty! Is it not superior to hypocrisy? – I wormed back into favour – each wriggle nurturing within the spite I harboured – until I became necessary to him, indispensable – he all the while despising me – Ha, ha, ha, ha! What triumph then when in his dying hours his papers were delivered to my hands, what sweet revenge – *And* opportunity! I prepared a new will and, to sign it, I engaged a master forger, my brother, who then emigrated; but lest he should return to blackmail me, I dared not destroy the real will but cached it in a secret place.

I'll have that cottage. And I take this pledge: Never again shall a drop of alcoholic liquor pass Phelim McGinty's lips until his mission is accomplished.

Scene Six

Interior cottage. An oil lamp burns. A want of comfort now. Alanna *will enter in a moment. She is a child.*

Arabella: Heaven, weigh not this poor creature down with woes beyond her strength to bear. Much I fear my suffering mother never can survive this night, and Edward comes not. And when he does arrive, how will he be? Oh misery! This agony of suspense. Heaven, aid this wife who is now six years a mother.

Enter Alanna.

Alanna: Dearest mother, do not cry.

Arabella: Forgive me, dear Alanna, but I sometimes cannot help it.

Alanna: I feel so sorry when you cry.

Arabella: There now: I am composed again.

Alanna: But when you cry it makes me want to cry too.

Arabella: My angel child! It is unjust of your mother to indulge her feelings. Have you eaten up your supper?

Alanna: *(Nods. Then:)* I cry too each night when father comes home late.

Arabella: When he arrives, smile, kiss him and then be very, very quiet.

Alanna: *(Nods.Then:)* But when I kiss him, Mother, his face is hot as fire or cold as ice.

Arabella: *(*'Hush'*)* – Is that a step?

Alanna: And why is he so pale, Mother?

Arabella: *(To herself; her voice is trembling)* I do not know.

Alanna: Mother, is he very ill?

Arabella*, to conceal her emotion, turns her back, shakes her head.*

What makes him so very ill, Mother?

Arabella: *(Choked sob)* He is perhaps unhappy with me? *(She is weeping, goes to the 'window' to conceal it)*

Alanna: Dear Grandmama too. Will she die tonight, Mother? Mother, will she die tonight?

Arabella: Father of Mercies, mercy! Be quiet, Alanna! Hush, my sweet innocence. I go to look in on her again. *(As she exits:)* Oh, Religion!

Alanna: Poor Mother: the colour drains from her face and her lips quiver. Oh Religion, sweet solace, support this family in these horrible, horrible trials.

A knock at the door.

Enter!

William *comes in. He is dressed for travelling and has his belongings in a roll.*

William: Alanna, darling! You're huge! You are! A foot taller and a power comelier every time I see you – Huge!

Alanna: Mr Earley.

William: Be your father not at home yet? *(She shakes her head)* And your mam?

Alanna *puts a finger to her lips and points.*

A-sittin' with the grandma. How is the poor creature?

Alanna: The nurse was here and shook her head, Father Harty held her hand and prayed in Latin.

William: Latin. The game is up then. She's kitted to take off.

Alanna: She's going up to heaven 'cause she's good. Father Harty told me so, and he never tells a falsehood, does he, 'cause he's good too?

William: Faith no, Alanna: His Reverence'd hardly taradiddle in a serious matter of that kind.

Arabella *comes in.*

Arabella: William!

William: Ma'am!

Arabella: Have you seen Edward?

William: Why, I saw him earlier outside the – in the village and he bade me to precede him – and that no one was to fret, mind! – and I'm sure he'll soon be here sure.

Arabella: Ever a good and loyal friend, William. Alanna, sit with your grandma.

Alanna: Yes, Mother. *(exit)*

Arabella: Was he –? How to frame my question. Is he sober?

William: Oh! he ...

Arabella: William?

William: Then I mustn't tell a lie, ma'am. He'd been taking – *some* – intoxicating liquor: I'd have to say that: I would. But, then, maybe not that much maybe: and maybe all'll maybe'll be well.

Arabella: Oh, heavens, if something could restore him to his former self. But you are all dressed up!

William: *(Proud of himself)* And somewhere to go!

Arabella: Oh?

Alanna *comes in for the bible and stays to register the reference to* Rencelaw *before going out again.*

William: I'm off to the big city in the post-chaise tonight with my little half-crazed sister Agnes. See what might be done about her malady. Sir Arden Rencelaw himself –

Arabella: Oh! –

William: Yes! – has took an interest and is gone before us on his steed.

Arabella: The world-famous philanthropist!

William: Friend to the unfortunate! –

Arabella: That great, good man!

William: Sure, he played the penny-whistle at your wedding sure! –

Arabella: I have done a likeness of him which hangs over our bed.

William: Whist!

Edward: *(Without)* 'Wine cures the gout and whiskey makes you sing.'

Arabella: 'Tis Edward!

Edward: *(Without)* 'Stout makes you fat, but –' Ow! Ow!

Arabella: He has fallen!

William: 'Tis Edward right enough.

Edward: 'But good brandy makes you king!' *(Entering)*

Arabella: Edward!

Edward: Who else should it be?

William: Ho, Ned!

Edward: Oh! You have company. Why, each time that I come home, is there a man here?

Arabella: He has come to –

Edward: So, it's stable-boys now!

Arabella: Edward! –

Edward: What is your purpose in having a servant here at this hour?

Arabella: Servant? – He is our friend –

Edward: Out of my house! –

Arabella: Edward! – Our last loyal friend!

Edward: Your friend, not my friend, I have no friends! –

Arabella: He has come to say goodbye.

Edward: Goodbye, farewell, good riddance!

Arabella: *(Whispers)* Go, William.

William: He's not himself, ma'am. When he sleeps it off him –

Edward: Still here! And *whispering* together? Leave, before I knock you down, Sir!

William: I'm going, Ned – I just called to –

Edward: Out of my house –

William: Farewell, friend –

Edward: Out of my house –

William: Fare you well. *(Exit)*

Edward: Farewell! *(Muttering:)* Farewell.

Arabella: Sit, my dear.

Edward: Do you have to tell me?

Arabella: Hush! Where were you?

Edward: Questions?!

Arabella: It's twenty-four hours since you crossed that threshold.

Edward: Why remind me? 'I've been drinking, I've been drinking where were wine and brandy good –'

Arabella: I'll fetch your supper – *(Moving to go out)*

Edward: 'And I'm thinking and I'm thinking how to get out of the wood!'

Arabella: *(Returning)* Oh hush, dearest, hush, oh hush –

Edward: Am I a child that I should remain silent in my own house?!

Arabella: Edward, Mother is –

Edward: This house that I could have sold tonight but for – Never mind! I sacrifice myself for everyone!

Arabella: *(To herself)* I must restrain myself. Our house, dear. Your daughter's house, yours and mine.

Alanna: *(Entering, coming to kiss him)* Father! Dear Father –

Edward: Keep off! I'm hot enough as it is. *(Muttering:)* This is what I come home to – 'Where were you?' 'Hush, dearest.' Five-six years now, I have borne these questions and complaints, endured food that you would not -

Arabella: *You* have borne, *you* have endured!

Edward: What's this?!

Arabella: *(To herself)* I *cannot* restrain myself.

Edward: What say you – *woman*?!

Arabella: Alanna, sit again with Grandmama.

Alanna: *(Whispers)* His face is cut, Mother. *(And exit)*

Arabella: You have borne, you have endured? And what have we borne and endured?

Edward: Insurrection!

Arabella: Without murmur! Maybe I, and *others*, were not nursed in the lap of luxury and so cannot mourn the comforts of ancestral halls, but have I not seen this once-warm home stripped and discomfited to a shell? Are we so unlike you – do *we* have no feelings – that we bear, endure, sacrifice, suffer nothing? Have we not had to watch you, day by day, sink to the footing of an outcast? Everywhere but here. Have we not been in receipt of your broken temper? Have I not seen your intelligence – everything about you! – coarsened and obscured by that infatuation of yours that my heart sickens to think upon, that my lips refuse to name?

Edward: Ho! Ho! Well – *Madam* – granted that you have all this – martyrdom – you have still the satisfaction of your sex – to *talk* about it.

Arabella: It pleases you, too, to cheaply wound with glibness.

Edward: Well then, if I be sunk so low and grown so hideous, pray, do not longer violate the delicacy of your feelings, but ... *(He indicates the door)*

Arabella: Leave you. *(To herself)*

Edward: And take with you your darling daughter.

Arabella: *(To herself)* How easy. No. Though you have brought us to this, though you have banished relations and every last friend from our home, though you draw the contempt of the world upon your head, though you are a mark for the good to grieve at, the vain to scoff, though abuse be levelled at you – and at us – you are still my daughter's father and my husband; though, in you, those designations – father and husband, both – are now coupled with the opprobrious, scurrilous and shameful epithet of ...

Edward: Complete your sentences. Of? ... *(Shouts:)* I-am-not-a-drunkard! It pleases you to punish with imputation my sensitivity. I-am-not-a-drunkard! It pleases you to impugn, with vices I do not possess, this unlucky character. Why? Because – Madam! – behind your persecution, the vice that you so carefully avoid to mention is my lack of means, which deprives you of the life of sloth that you would lead, which deprives you of the silks, feathers and frippery that your vanity craves!

Arabella: *(To herself)* My vanity.

Edward: Hah! I have hit it.

Arabella: Do you believe, Sir, that only vanity has hunger, that only empty pride of dress has appetite? Are these the only wants and cravings? Know you how the food for your supper was procured? How-was-it-procured? By what magic came it here? How did I come by the money?

Edward: *(Dark, threatening; suspicion/jealousy)* By what means? How was it procured – How?!

Arabella: For 'tis long since I received financial help from you.

Edward: How? – Tell me! – Speak! How came you by the money? Satisfy me or, by heaven and by hell's damnation, you shall know all about it from me! *(His fist is raised)*

Arabella: *(Holds out her hand)* You do not even notice its absence. Your ring. Your ring bought your supper. Your ring provided you with the money you so artfully took from the box before leaving here yesterday. The ring that was fixed upon my finger by a gentle, loving, honourable, young man called Edward, was wrested from its holy place to buy a little food and to purchase intoxication for a degraded, selfish drunkard. *(She is weeping)*

He backs away, aghast. She continues to weep. The following is very gentle, in whispers, or little more than whispers.

Edward: Bella.

Arabella: Dearest?

Edward: Arabella.

Arabella: Dearest?

Edward: All reveals your constancy, my disgrace.

Arabella: No. No.

Edward: No. No.

Arabella: Dearest, dearest, do not think that.

Edward: No. No.

Arabella: Forgive me for speaking thus.

Edward: No. No.

Arabella: Besides, all is past now.

Edward: No. No. I must leave.

Arabella: No, Edward, my adored.

Edward: No.

Alanna *is entering.*

Arabella: I'll do anything – I shall enlist aid from – *somewhere.* There must be – *someone* – to whom we can apply for help!

Edward: I must leave forever.

Arabella: No –

Alanna: Father –

Arabella: My husband!

Edward: Father, husband? *(He shakes his head, 'No')* Curse me as your destroyer.

Arabella: I shall follow wherever you go!

Edward: No. Forget this unfortunate man who never will forget you! *(He rushes out)*

Alanna: *(Running out)* Father!

Arabella: *(Follows)* Edward!

Alanna: Faather!

Arabella: Edwaard!

Alanna: Faaather!

Arabella: Edwaaard!

Their voices continue, off, growing more distant and becoming distorted by the howling wind that has risen and that continues to the end of the scene.

The stage is empty. A breeze is catching the flame in the oil-lamp, which, in turn, is casting shadows about the room; a nimbus appears to be forming round a shadow, creating – could it be? – the figure of an old man. And the ancient Mother, *in shroud/nightdress, is now entering, her arms reaching out to the haloed, ghostly thing:*

Mother: Bartholomew! … I'm coming! … We are together again … Take me! …

The oil lamp flickers and gutters to its last. Music.

ACT TWO

Scene One

City street/alleyway. On the ground, there is what looks like a heap of rags and litter.

Rencelaw: Another year has come and gone. A new day has passed its noontide. Our hero awakens.

The rags and litter have stirred: Edward *slowly sitting up. His condition has deteriorated. He looks terrible.*

He sleeps now on the street. What his morning prayer? His thought? Feelings? Everything for him now starts and finishes in a bottle. City life speeds the downhill course.

Now Two Loafers, *one each side of* Edward, *are waking up with headaches and what-have-you.*

Loafer 1: Oooooofff – ah-hah-haaa! Does I need a drink?

Loafer 2: Does yous need a drink? Oooooofff – ah-hah-haaa!

Edward: Is't tomorrow?

Loafer 1: Does he need a – Ah, ha, ha, ha, ha!

Leading to a bout of phlegmatic coughing-and-laughing from the three of them.

Rencelaw: Can habitual intoxication stand as epitome of every crime? Is't too harsh to make such claim? A Roman stoic – regarded as my near equal for imperturbable temper and balanced judgement – seeking to fix stigma on the man who had ruined his sister, called him not knave, destroyer, debauchee or villain, but wreaked every odium with one word, drunkard. And is it not at least debatable that all the vices that stain our nature may find ready germination in that state, and wait but little time to sprout forth in pestilential rankness?

But I leave perusal of the thought with you, for at this point in the narrative I am away in Switzerland, enlisting the opinion of Dr Carl Freung in the matter of Agnes Earley's malady, which, surprisingly, was proving recalcitrant to my solo efforts at renovation. (*To himself*) A pretty girl. Don'tcha know. *(And exits)*

A woman – first Floozie *– oldish, down-and-out, is entering, followed by* McGinty. *She points at* Edward*:*

Floozie: Would that bowsie be your man, Sir?

Edward: I feel most shockingly.

Floozie: Him, round here, we do call Lord Teddy.

McGinty *gives her a coin and she retires.*

McGinty: There's the drunken vagrant.

Edward: I am quite on fire.

Loafer 1: Cheer up, Neddy, you'll soon be dead!

Loafer 2: Do we have the price of a drink?

Edward: 'Tis a burning question.

They laugh and cough.

McGinty: With two bright friends. And by the looks of him, he has nothing left to offer by way of resistance to what I want.

Loafer 1: *(has produced a cosh)* Time to go to work, we need money.

Loafer 2: There'll be more where the last came from.

Loafer 1: Yous stay put, Lord Teddy, mind our furnishings and effects. Joe and me'll take a turn down the docks, a liner from abroad gets in today. *(*Loafers *exit)*

McGinty: Now for my design on him. *(He crosses, affecting to be unaware of* Edward*'s presence)*

Edward: Sir! Sir!

McGinty: Someone calls?

Edward: Charity or a copper – Hither, Sir! – for a broken-down soldier.

McGinty: Why, certainly, my poor, brave veteran. Here's something. Oh! Sir! can it be you, Sir? Master Kilcullen Sir, luminary, exceller, decoration of the Kilcullen family and empire?

Edward: Beg pardon?

McGinty: Never!

Edward: McGinty?

McGinty: Why, by all that's happy, it is my young master!

Edward: What's left of me.

McGinty: I don't see you much altered. A stitch – maybe two – about the elbows. But you can always count on my friendship for a little charity. Here we are. *(Offers money)*

Edward: Well … *(He hesitates; a bit embarrassed)*

McGinty: Yes, take it! After all, we are fellow villagers.

Edward: Well … Fellow villagers you say? *(Takes money)*

McGinty: Yes! You once from the big house, I from the little.

Edward: Ha, ha, ha!

McGinty: Ha, ha, ha!

Edward: Dare I ask …

McGinty: He's going to ask about his wife and child. Young Sir, Sir?

Edward: Have you seen them?

McGinty: Sir? Oh! Your wife and child. *(Aside)* I shall not tell him they are in this very town in search of him. They are doing charmingly! Exceeding well and happy, you'll be glad to hear! Your strange conduct, your – migrating – from them attracted the sympathy of the gentle folk about the area and your wife is given an abundance of washing and sewing. She is quite a favourite, and her pretty face helps, mmm! Never better! Doing famously!

Edward: She is happy then. *(His head is bowed)*

McGinty: As the day is long. She's as merry as a cricket, brisk and busy as a bee.

Edward: Well, I ought to be glad of it. And I am. And that she thinks no more of me.

McGinty: Oh she thinks of you!

Edward: *(eagerly)* Does she – does she?

McGinty: Oh, yes! She says, what paradox! misfortune turning blessing. She says she never, ever would have realised the curious friendship of those dear hearts and gentle neighbours had you not left her.

Edward: Did she say that? *(His head is bowed again)*

McGinty: And more! *(To himself)* Further cripple him and make him more amenable to my scheme. Young Sir! She says she pities you.

Edward: *Pity?*

McGinty: What else?!

Edward: Well, that is, that is – Cursed taverns not yet open! Well, that is very kind of her, I'm sure.

McGinty: The world deals a tinch unfairly with you, Master Edward?

Edward: It treats me ill, McGinty.

McGinty: It misuses a little?

Edward: It abuses me!

McGinty: And what remedy for the casualty? There is but one. If the world ill-treats, be revenged upon the world.

Edward: Revenged? But how?

McGinty: Have a drink.

Edward: *(A beat, and)* Ha, ha, ha!

McGinty: Ha, ha, ha! But, hold! Charity buys but poor revenge, retaliation requires higher fee than what is in your fist. I have it! Do you by chance still have about your person the deeds to that old cottage in the village?

Edward: Here. *(In his pocket)*

McGinty: Fortunate! And I a purse in mine, containing a full two hundred pounds. All that is required is for the document to be signed.

Edward: But you are aware as I that the document requires two signatures.

McGinty: Easily resolved! You are an excellent penman. How your dear father boasted of your hand when comparing it to my scrawl.

Edward: The plaudits for calligraphy and Vere Foster Prize I won at school so pleased Papa.

McGinty: There you are then, show your skill! Sign your noble name with flourish and, in her fashion, the name of the wife who pities you, and you may laugh vengeance in the world's face.

Edward: *(Has the document in his hand)* Ought I?

McGinty: Yes.

Edward: Should I?

McGinty: Yes! Come over here and do the signing.

Off, cheering has been growing in the streets. Loafers, *old* Floozie, *other* Floozies *– as available – and* Bartender *are entering, like the outlying members of a welcoming throng, laughing at and cheering someone, which distracts* Edward.

Edward: Has a war been truced?

McGinty: Yes – But let's –

Edward: Parade? St Patrick's Day?

McGinty: Yes-yes – But let's proceed with the transaction. An assemblage to welcome home that old duffer and affecter, Arden Rencelaw. *(Gives his pen to* Edward*)*

Edward: What! Do you mean Sir Arden Rencelaw?

McGinty: Yes, that old humbug – Come!

Rencelaw, *as if in an open carriage, is seen over the heads of those present, acknowledging the adoring populace.*

Edward: Do you mean the princely merchant, the noble philanthropist, who in disguise played tin-whistle at my wedding? Whose life-size picture hangs upon the bedroom wall at home, an astonishing likeness done in needle-work stitches by my own wife's hand! Do you refer to Sir Arden Rencelaw, the poor man's friend, the orphan's benefactor, the great humanitarian reformer, on whose opinion the State awaits with bated breath, upon whose every sacred word the Church hangs, blessed?

McGinty: *(To himself)* Hot air.

Edward: Whose very presence – even at far proximity – can inspire greatness in others?

McGinty: Blether, blarney, twaddle, malarky. *(He's not impressed by* Edward *or* Rencelaw*)*

Edward: Pardon?

McGinty: Talk!

Edward: Exactly! And talk does not put potatoes on the table of the foolish husband, does it, who stays in bed for half the morning cultivating his wife?! So, you see! *(Moves away, calls to the parade:)* Hooray for Sir Arden! *(Returns)* Did you come here by any chance, McGinty, to bribe me with this so-called charity? Did you mean, Sir, that I should commit a forgery with this? *(Pen)* For shame! Shocking! Out and out with you for a villain and a coward that you dare propose such baseness to my father's son!

McGinty: *(To himself)* A final fiddle-faddling puff of self-indulgent righteousness.

Edward: I would sooner perish on a dunghill.

McGinty: Would you?

Edward: Take back your poisoned quill! *(He joins the others, cheering, laughing. 'Hooray, shipmates, hooray!')*

McGinty: A last lickspittling token to virtue. The game is up. He returned the villain's 'poisoned quill', did he return the 'so-called charity' was given him? Yes, the ember may flicker but, anon, when he is moistened and burns for drenching, we shall see his true passion flare. My aspiration will fulfil itself before the night is out – with *bonus.* The wife – for is not she too a Kilcullen? – will be possessed.

Music. The lighting has changed during the above, it is now night-time and the cheering spectators from the street are raucous in the tavern, calling for drinks.

Scene Two

City tavern. McGinty *is here, too, watching, encouraging. The* Bartender *is a busy man.*

Bartender: Yes sir, yes sir, yes sir, yes sir!

Loafer 1: Whiskey there! –

Edward: Brandy here! –

Loafer 1: And for you, Joe? –

Loafer 2: A rum-rum-rum!

Bartender: Whiskey there, brandy here and a rum-rum-rum-rum-rum!

Loafer 1: Whiskey!

Edward: Brandy!

Loafer 2: Rum-rum-rum!

Bartender: Yes sir, yes sir, coming up!

Loafer 1: And for the ladies?!

Bartender: Three teas! With cakes or muffins, girls?

Floozies: And we'll pay you back with crumpet! *(Laughter)*

Floozie 1: *(Old whore)* I'll have what killed Goliath!

Floozies 2 & 3: A gin-sling! *(Laughter)*

Bartender: Steady on, steady on, don't raise a row in a decent house!

Laughter, jeers, cheers. Toasts:

Edward: Here's to the maiden of bashful fifteen!

Loafer 1: Here's to the widow of fifty!

Bartender: Here! give that to her highness, Pock Alley's Queen! *(A drink to be passed to* Floozie 1*)*

Edward: To parchment-and-ink face, Sir Thrifty! *(Mocking* McGinty*)*

McGinty: Here's to this lass with a bosom of snow! *(Moving/easing* Floozie 2 *towards* Edward*)*

Loafer 1: And to this one, brown as a berry!

Edward: Here's to the wife with a face full of woe! *(To* Floozie 2*)*

Floozie 1: Here's to myself that gets merry!

Edward*, above, has drawn* Floozie 2 *to himself. Now he is backing away from her – he shakes his head as if to wake up: She looks, strangely, like* Arabella.

McGinty: *(Whispers to* Floozie 2*)* Follow him, lass, follow him, lass – I'll warrant she'll prove an excuse for a glass.

Edward: 'Nother round, another round!

Bartender: Yes sir, yes sir, yes sir, yes sir!

Loafer 1: Whiskey there! –

Edward: Brandy here! –

Loafer 1: And for you, Joe? –

Loafer 2: A rum-rum-rum!

Bartender: Whiskey there, brandy here and a rum-rum-rum-rum-rum!

Loafer 1: And for the ladies?!

Floozie 1: I'll have what killed Goliath!

Floozies 2 & 3: A gin-sling!

Bartender: Steady on, steady on, don't raise a row!

Laughter, cheers, jeers.

Edward: Come, come, everybody! Is someone dead, this somebody's funeral, someone going to preach – sermon?! Come, come!

Floozie 2: Then sing us a song!

Floozie 1: I'll sing a song! –

Loafer 1: No, he'll sing a song! –

Edward: Neither of you shall sing a song! –

Floozie 1: *(Singing, raucously:)* 'Years ago out in the wilds of Australia –' ! –

Edward: I'm master here! – Silence! -

Bartender: No quarrelling, no quarrelling! –

Edward: He shall sing a song – Joe!

Loafer 2: 'Here's a health to the King and a lasting peace, /To faction an end, to wealth increase, /Come let us drink while we have breath.'

All: 'For there's no drinking after death'

Loafer 2: 'And he that will this health deny'

All: 'Down among the dead men /Down among the dead men'

Loafer 2: 'Down, down, down, down'

All: 'Down among the dead men let him lie.'

Edward*, revelling, sings the second verse: (He is drawn to* Floozie 2*, his eyes are glazed, he circles her, he dances with her?)*

Edward:

In smiling Bacchus' joys I'll roll,
Deny no pleasure to my soul,
Let Bacchus' health round briskly move,
For Bacchus is a friend to love,
And he that will this health deny …

All: 'Down among the dead men let him lie.' *(They are amused at* Edward*'s attention to*Floozie 2*)*

Edward: Your name please.

Floozie 2: Can you not guess?

Edward: I should not like, Miss, actually, to hazard one, just now.

Floozie 2: Why it's …Prudence, of course. *(Laughter)*

Floozie 3: Mine's Patience!

Floozie 1: And mine's Chastity!

Laughter, together with Edward*'s inordinate pleasure (and relief that* Floozie 2 *isn't called Arabella) and he keeps repeating the name:*

Edward: Prudence! Prudence!

Loafer 1: Lord Teddy's made a conquest!

Edward: Everybody, her name is Prudence!

Floozie 2: And yours, Sir?

Edward: Temperance!

All: Ha, ha, ha, ha, ha, ha, ha …!

Floozies:

> May love and wine their rites maintain,
> And their united pleasures reign,
> While Bacchus' treasure crowns the board,
> We'll sing the joys that both afford,
> And they that wont with us comply –

Others: 'Down among the dead men let them lie!'

Edward: This calls for another round! Bartender, another round!

Bartender: *(A beat, and)* You've perhaps the money in your purse?

Edward: Perhaps I have – Ha, ha, ha!

Bartender: Then perhaps I can see it so that neither of us is in doubt.

Floozies: *(With others, as appropriate; quietly)* 'Down among the dead men, down among the dead men …'

Edward *has searched himself: he has no money. (He looks at* Loafer 1 *who, too, is broke)*

Edward: *(a plea)* Sir, pour me a brandy …One more …One…An ale then…

Floozies: *(And others)* 'Down, down, down, down'

Edward: I must have a drink.

Floozies: *(And others)* 'Down among the dead men let him lie.'

Bartender *is unforthcoming.*

Edward: *(To himself)* I must have a drink.

And McGinty *comes forward with his pen in one hand and a large roll of money in the other.* Edward *takes the document from his pocket and the pen from* McGinty.

Edward: Is this the end then? And that I am an object of pity to my once adoring wife. The friendship of others has made up my loss. I am a wretch with but one resource: Liquor.

He is poised to sign the document; he pauses for the briefest moment to half-register a call from (the now near-dark or the dark) behind him:

Loafer 1: Prudence awaits you!

And he signs, gives the document to McGinty *who, in turn, gives* Edward *the large roll of money.* McGinty *leaves. And* Edward *goes to the counter and puts the roll of money into the* Bartender*'s hand.*

Edward: You will, I know, Sir, be good enough to tell me when that is drunk.

Music

Scene Three

A wretched garret. A single lamp burns dimly, by which Arabella *sits, sewing 'slop-work', an old shawl about her shoulders.* Alanna *is on a straw bed, pretending to be asleep.*

Arabella: Where is he on this very bitter night? In vain have I made every effort and enquiry to gain tidings of his whereabouts. *(She is prey to her imagination:)* He is alone and he is ill! Even to enlist the help of Lawyer McGinty, whose offices I chanced upon today when abroad the streets in search of a few shavings. He is fallen down and no one comes to his assistance! These shirts must be handed in by eight. My industry will be repaid by a miserable two shillings. He is the inmate of a prison! But then, at least, with that little money there shall be some kind of food upon the table for my child.

Alanna: Ah me alas, I am so cold! But I shall not let dear mother know for she is careworn as it is, faint with hunger and fatigued from work. But in the morning I shall be able to warm myself at Mrs. O'Brien's fire downstairs. Little Dennis, her son, with whom I sometimes play, told me that I should. The mother of that little boy is blessed.

Arabella: My sweet lamb sleeps, and sleep offers some relief. *(Her imagination again :)* The earth is already closed over him! *(She steals to the bed and covers* Alanna *with her shawl)* Still, that ever I should see his child thus.

A clock chimes one. Returns to her work:

One o' clock, my work not yet near finished. Merciful heaven, restore to me my Edward and I shall pay any price, bear every burden, accept whatever ill that ... that can ... that can be ... heaped ... upon me. *(She is nodding to sleep)*

Alanna *watches, and to encourage her mother's sleep she begins to sing, softly:*

> Oh Mother-my-love, if you'll give me your hand
> And go where I ask you to wander,
> I'll lead us away to a beautiful land –
> The dreamland that's waiting out yonder.

Arabella *is asleep.* Alanna *has tiptoed from the bed, and returns the shawl to her mother's shoulders:*

Ah, Mother, you tried to trick your little darling by giving me your shawl.

She takes up the work – the shirts – and she begins sewing them, one eye on her mother.

Arabella *stirs in her sleep.* Alanna *sings:*

> I'll rock you to sleep on a silver-dew stream,
> And sing you asleep when you're weary,
> And no one shall know of our beautiful dream
> But you and your own little dearie.

Arabella: Edward. *(In her sleep)*

Alanna: We shall find him, Mother.

Arabella: Edward. *(In her sleep)*

Alanna: We shall find him. With the help of God, and the aid of my secret friend to whom I shall write yet again. *(And sings:)*

> So Mother-my-love, let me take your dear hand
> And away through the starlight we'll wander,

Away through the mists to the beautiful land –
The Dreamland that's waiting out yonder.

A knock at the door.

(Whispers to herself) Father!

Arabella: *(Awakened)* Who can that be?

Alanna: It is father!

Arabella: Ah, that it were he! *(Calls)* Yes?

And McGinty *enters.*

McGinty: Ah, the lovely Mrs Kilcullen! – Good evening, good evening!

Arabella: Sir! *(Curtseys:)* Good evening! But – *Evening*?

McGinty: I saw your light as I was passing, remembered your address from our meeting today and friends are welcome at all hours and seasons?

Arabella: 'Tis an untimely hour to visit, Sir, but if you have come with ought of Edward's whereabouts, even the slenderest of tidings, you would be welcome at any time.

McGinty: Ah, the dear child! Here's a sixpence for you, take my hat and cane to the next room and wait there.

Alanna: There is no other room.

McGinty: Hmm! Not the most commodious for the interview I have in mind. May I suggest immediate alternative accommodation for the two of us?

Arabella: Heaven help us, where could we go?

McGinty: To a little – nest? You must know that I'm a man of means and can supply – the feathers?

Arabella: Nest, feathers?

McGinty: A reward for your compliance.

Arabella: Ah! You refer to our cottage in the village. How we long for return to our home! But we made a vow to remain in this poor place until Edward is discovered.

McGinty: So be it then!

Arabella: What news, Sir, of him?

McGinty: Young, young, *beautiful* lady, I find this infatuation of yours most strange!

Arabella: Sir? Do you find love strange?

McGinty: Indeed I do! And it would appear, there is no cure for it but marriage. 'Tis very strange. And stranger still, since the love-object in the case in point is a foolish, no-good, indolent profligate.

Arabella: Sir, is it of my husband that you speak?

McGinty: I mean no offence, but of – who else?!

Arabella: Then he is alive!

McGinty: And kicking!

Arabella: Thank heavens!

McGinty: Thank heavens yes! And does charmingly in a circle of companions, whose company, clearly, he prefers to yours.

She takes a step backwards.

I mean not to distress, but a woman, practical as she is beautiful – with the calculating foresight to have her interests regularised on legal documents? – should like to know the facts in order to take further 'dancing' steps. And to apprise you more of the company he keeps: with the male half, his revels are of one kind; tired of that, the sociability of the other half consoles.

Arabella: *(Another step backwards; and a whisper:)* Oh Sir, what do you say to me?

McGinty: I mean not to distress, my dear, but the things I speak of have always been, and will be, while the two sexes exist, let alone where there are drunkards on the one side and harlots on the other.

Arabella: *(A whisper)* Oh Sir, this cannot be, oh Sir, do not break my heart.

McGinty: My dear young lady, I fear it is so, and you know it is so, and a woman of your intelligence will begin immediately to salvage her one big mistake in life. Give me your hand.

She complies. She appears transfixed by him. He strokes her hand:

Soft. Soft.

Arabella: What mistake?

McGinty: Choice of poor man.

Arabella: What? Nothing of what you say is true. *(She comes to; snatches her hand away)*

McGinty: Come, come, my dear, this part of the scene is unnecessary!

Arabella: You lie! You calumniate my husband – I know you do! – You lie like a rascal! – and now you slander me – and before a child! Gaze on her features where famine has already set its seal, look on this hapless woman who brought her into the world, then, if you have heart, speak further insult to us!

McGinty: Hah, the heart! A little red dripping barrel of cruelty.

Arabella: I love my husband! I love him the more because he *is* poor, forsaken and reviled. It is why I follow him!

McGinty: He laughs at you in his drunken ribaldry!

Arabella: *(Tearfully)* False! That is false – He would never laugh at me! False! False! The fault of my husband, the *only* fault, is his intemperance – Terrible, terrible, I acknowledge! But it is an illness! Call it a weakness, if you will, but it is one that has assailed the finest and most sensitive intellects of mankind: men who, though prostrated with the affliction, would, to the very last, scorn you and your kind – *your* sickness! – your moral deformity and warped philosophy!

McGinty: I must say it is a good game you play.

Arabella: Game?!

McGinty: Yes. And you are proficient in the craft of tears. *(He takes her hand)*

Arabella: *(Snatches her hand away)* You are contemptible.

McGinty: Ha, ha, ha!

Arabella: Now you reveal the real purpose in your coming here. Get out!

McGinty: You know it better than I: a woman cannot have purity and intelligence, both.

Arabella: You scoundrel!

McGinty: Rapscallion!

Arabella: Ruffian!

McGinty: Scapegrace, slubberdegullion! –

Arabella: Knave! –

McGinty: Ha, ha, ha! You are young and you know it, beautiful – you know it – I desire you, you will yield to me and you know it –

Arabella: Unhand me! You are despicable and you *don't* know it! But *know* it, how much I despise you, *know* it that my husband, covered in mire, drunk at my feet –

McGinty: Perishing on a dunghill! –

Arabella: Unhand, unhand me! –

Alanna: Help! Help!

McGinty: You verge too close to insolence now. Remember your circumstances – Remember it is late, you are helpless and unfriended –

Alanna: *(This time, calling out of the window)* Help! Help! Oh, won't someone come to our aid?

Voice: *(Without)* Holloo!

Alanna: Help! Help! –

Voice: Holloo! Holloo!

Alanna: Mr Earley! Mr Earley! It is Mr Earley.

William: *(Rushes in)* Mary and Joseph! It's Mrs Kilcullen's little darling, Alanna. And Mrs Kilcullen! And howdydo! what have we here? Oh bo, bo, bo, bo, bo: think of the devil and you meet his first cousin!

McGinty *trying to hide or slope away.*

Ho, Squire, you lizard! *(Throws* McGinty *about)* Ho, Mr Honey! What's the lowest you'll take for your skin? Shall I turn auctioneer and knock you down to this bidder? – or this one? – Or here's a higher one!

McGinty: I'm a respectable man –

William: You a man? Nature made a mistake!

McGinty: Strike me and I'll sue you!

William: Strike me, but if I don't set your paddles going all-fired-quick!

McGinty: I have two witnesses!

William: Out you get or see if I don't play The Wind that Shakes the Barley on your organ of rascality!

Throws him out, down the stairs.

McGinty: *(Without; tumbling)* Ow-wow-wow-wow-wow!

William: *(Finds* McGinty*'s hat)* Well, I declare: a silk hat for a man like that!

McGinty: *(Without)* You'll find I have not done with you!

William: Nor I with you! *(Deftly aiming and pitching the hat out at* McGinty*)*

McGinty: *(Without)* Ow!

Arabella: William, ever friend!

William: It did ill–behove me, ma'am, to dust him further in your presence.

Arabella: But how came you upon us so opportunely?

William: Well now, that be a long tale. But mind you of Sir Arden Rencelaw?

Arabella: He is seldom from my mind.

Alanna: We keep his picture.

She takes the lamp to the wall, they follow, and we see Sir Arden's *life-size 'picture' on it.*

Arabella: I would not be without it.

Alanna: We pray to it as we do to God.

Arabella: For anyone who knows Sir Arden Rencelaw wishes to know more of Sir Arden Rencelaw.

William: A truer word was never spoken, ma'am. Well, on account he's been away in Switzerland with my little half-crazed sister Agnes – the same Agnes, you'll be glad to hear, is now – well, by Sir Arden's remarkable lights – is now but tuppence short of the shilling, but, dang me, if by my lights, there isn't more than tuppence worth of air still getting in up there. *(i.e., air getting into* Agnes' *head)* Howandever, he did only on his return today get your letter.

Arabella: Letter, William? What letter, I wrote no letter?! *(What a puzzle)*

Alanna: Please, Mother: I hope it does not vex you, but this picture has become my secret friend and inspired by the noble features delineated in it, I took it on myself to write entreaty to Sir Arden on our behalf.

Arabella: Oh, my child, it does not vex me. *(To* William*)* And he sent you to us?

William: Aye, that be so.

Arabella: And you have found Edward!

William: Aye, well, that not be so.

Arabella: William?

William: Then I mustn't tell a lie, ma'am. We haven't found him but, even if we do, by whatever accident Sir Arden's got to know of your Edward's present condition …

Arabella: Speak!

William: All efforts now to save his life may have come too late.

Arabella *faints.*

Scene Four

Agnes *appears in the transition, to gaze as one at prayer at* Sir Arden*'s 'picture'.*

Agnes: His features. His features.

She carries a crucifix, which, now, she remembers, guiltily:

Oh Christ's too, oh our Blessed Saviour's too, of course, too, oh I wouldn't say otherwise, oh Christ no,

Christ knows! But … *(wistfully) his* features. Don'tcha know.

We are in the Sir Arden Rencelaw Foundation. Agnes *wears an institutional-type dress and she is now scrubbed clean. She appears quite dreamy – some might say love-lorn or, indeed, scatty. But she pulls herself together to get on with the business of the play.*

For three days now are we returned and for three days he has been abroad the city streets … (*She forgets her purpose*) And I miss his daily instruction. *(She assumes Rencelaw's bearing and tone:*) 'With good economy, Miss Agnes, few need be poor.' Without economy, Sir Arden, none can be rich.

Rencelaw: (*The 'picture' behind her speaks)* Everything has a beginning, Miss Agnes, except?

Agnes: Except God.

Rencelaw: Don'tcha know.

She pulls herself together.

Agnes: For three days now we are returned and for three days he has been abroad the city streets, assiduously preaching temperance, and in desperate search of another soul to save: that of Young Edward Kilcullen. *(Beat)* And I miss him. He says – with look I know not what to make of –

Rencelaw: You may address me, Miss Agnes, by my first name.

Agnes: *(Silently/whispered:)* Arden. But I am much too shy.

Rencelaw: Address me by my first name –

Agnes: He says –

Rencelaw: Don'tcha know.

Agnes: Can't. And I am very much improved, he says, and how pleased his countenance that I respond to his tuition.

Rencelaw: Cabbage and carrots were unknown before?

Agnes: 1545.

Rencelaw: It would take 27,000 spiders to produce?

Agnes: It would take 27,000 spiders to produce one pound of web.

And I weep with delight when he gives me a smile.

Rencelaw: But one last mist remains –

Agnes: He says, that I must –

Rencelaw: Sunder and disperse! *(And he's gone)*

Agnes: And I tremble with fear lest he frown. *(She is lost. She grows agitated:)* Brake, fern, cypress dell where – no, cabbage, carrots, cypress dell where – no, one pound of spiders to make 27,000 webs – no, no, no! *(Repeat, as necessary – her mind is reeling : A half-swoon perhaps)*

A strange fancy keeps forming in my brain: it flits across my mind like a half-forgotten dream : oh what can it be? A remembrance vague of a moonlit night when I'd concealed myself to observe the strange behaviour of the sane section of mankind ... *(Swoons into a trance and, like one possessed, she begins to speak in a male bass:)* Wait. Wait ... Night. The moping owl falls silent.

The shadows submit, and now, clean-bathed in their lunar lover's tide, hide under the trees. Night holds its breath... Lo! a man steals across the sward from a little house – No, wait. He steals from the big house, *brick* house, *brick* house. And neath his great black coat he conceals ... What can it be?... Wait. A box, tin box, tin box and now he buries it in the earth, tin box, in cypress dell, midst brake and fern, by the old moss-covered wall of – of St. Scooteen's Monastery! And 'tis honest Lawyer McGinty!... Phew! I have sundered the last mist. Oh, he will be pleased. *(Silently/whispered:)* Arden! Arden! *(And, as she runs off:)* The will – ha, ha, ha! ...

Scene Five

A stable or outhouse. It is dark but nearing dawn. Edward *is on the floor, delirious. He is without coat, hat, shoes; the clothes he wears are torn and dirty. He is in 'the jigs'. At first, perhaps, he is quiet; staring eyes; slowly pulling up his knees and pulling back his bare feet, to protect them from something. His innocent horror. It is as if a tide is coming towards him. He thinks he has escaped, that this 'tide' is moving past him, but – 'Ah!' – something on his arm which he flicks off. But – 'Ah!' – another on his thigh. Another and another, in his hair, his mouth – 'Ah!' 'Thwuh!' ... An infestation of creepie-crawlies have come for him. They are on his hands, around and in between his fingers. And he cannot yet bring himself to roar. They are making low-pitched sounds – like bees that have invaded his skull;*

they pant like dogs needing water … They are all over him. Now, a growing roar:

Edward: OoooOOOO ! MamaaaAAA! MamaaaAAA! Send them away, send them away, stop them, stop them …!

The tide recedes. (Made up of crawling Floozies *perhaps and others – as available – but* Floozies *in particular)*

What hideous place is this, where am I? …Is it hell? … Dream? … Does dream occur after one is dead? … Is it night? … Morn? Coming morn, coming night? … I wanted day but, if it come, what shall I do with light? How to hide my face away from … from me? … If it be night, how to bear again the unleashed terrors of Dark's enhancing powers? … Ah! dawn spreads a rosy hue over night time's troubled skies: the stars at last are released from their ticking spasms, but, ah me! It is morn.

Now, again, he tries to make himself smaller, to hide, protect himself. This time it is an invasion of snakes. He whimpers:

No … No … Off … Off me …Away … Get away … Take them away … Off! Off! *(He appears to be hurtling them away, but one snake is persistent)* NoooOOO! Take it off me! Take it – MamaaaAAA – get it off me!... Mama, it tightens – how it coils – Tightens! … Dash, dash, dash you to a pulp against the wall!

Snakes – Figures – retiring.

I breathe again.

Figures returning. (This time, upright, standing, or nearly so)

noOOOOO! I am awake – Mama, Papa, tell them! Dreams – you are dreams – you are shockingly bad dreams! Will you return upon me when my eyes – See! – are gaping wide? *(Pleads:)* Please you, leave? Please?

Figures *draw back. Every fibre of him is shaking.*

I should not be so stricken were I in these hands to hold a glass ... Nor so fearful, despairing, astonished, or ashamed ... Ashamed? *(He shakes his head, 'No', wearily)*

A figure enters, a Man. *(He will, later, turn out to be real)* Edward *watches him, at first suspiciously.*

Man: Who left the door open? Where is the horse? Where in blazes is my horse?

Edward: I say, you there!

Man: Who's there?!

Edward: Yes, you there, Landlord Tubbs from our village, pour us a drink!

Man: Who's there, I say!

Edward: It is I, Young Edward Kilcullen!

Man: *(Assuming a new voice)* Ah, the scape-gallows, Kilcullen!

Figures: Ha, ha, ha, ha, ha, ha! *(Coming forward)*

Edward: Scape-gallows – Ha, ha, ha! – Good old Tubbs, ever fond of a jest – You and I have long been friends – Don't draw back! pour us another and be quick about it!

Floozie 1: And the devil's to pay!

Figures: Ha, ha, ha, ha, ha!

Edward: But it is I, Edward Kilcullen, a respected worthy!

Loafer 1: You were that once, Teddy!

Floozie 1: And so was Lucifer!

Figures: Ha, ha, ha, ha, ha!

Edward: Fetch him here! – Tubbs, Tubbs, I am ill, faint, my brain I think's on fire – Give me a drink!

Man: Ho, ho, ho, ho, ho, ho, ho!

Edward: Think how I was when I first entered your shop! Make amends!

Floozie 2: Make amends for what, Lord Teddy Temperance?

Edward: Prudence! assist me –

Floozie 1: You had your senses –

Floozie 2: Did he invite you in? –

Loafer 1: You walked in the man's door –

Man: Did I invite you in? –

Figures: Ha, ha, ha, ha, ha ...!

Edward: *(Angrily, bitterly; over-lapping them)* HA, HA, HA, HA, HA! Does hell send cards of invitation forth to its fires of torment? Curse you, Tubbs – Curse you all! If it had not been for you and your infernal shops I had been still a man! *(He lies back, whimpering)*

Rencelaw: *(Light up on* Rencelaw*)* The foul shops – Dens! – where pockets are plundered, where death and disease are dealt in tumblers – with little thought from the noxious purveyors than to count the profits of the till; from whence goes forth the blast of ruin on our land, stealing and withering the beauty and intelligence of our youth – Youth! Our future! Our promise, pride, joy, our hope, turned into a generation of animals! The waves of that direful sickness extending, leaving none unaffected, wounding to futility the loving relatives, filling the mother's, sister's, brother's hearts with anguish, the widows' with grief, orphans cursed, blighting ambition and all that is glorious in man and casting him from his high estate! *(Fade on* Rencelaw*)*

Edward: And making of him such as I? *(He chuckles, bitterly?)*

Man *enters, as before:*

Man: Where, in nature, can my horse have gone?

Edward: *(Quietly)* Here is your horse.

Man: Who's there? ... Who's there, I say!

Edward: You common poisoner! It is I, Young Edward Kilcullen. *(He springs on* Man *and takes him by the throat)*

Man: Murder! Murder!

Edward: I have a claim on you now, a deadly claim –

Man: Release – release me –

Edward: So, a drink, one drink, a single glass –

Man: Let go your hold –

Edward: Or I shall have your last breath!

Man: Help! I am choking! Police! Arrrrrgh!

William: *(Without)* Holloo! Holloo! *(Rushing in:)* What goes here?

He pulls Edward *off* Man. Edward *falls back.* Man *rushes off, calling*

Man: Police! Police! …

William: *(Shocked)* Edward? Mary and Joseph! Young master, friend, can this be you?

Edward: Shhhh! Hush, she sleeps.

William: Edward, don't you know who I am?

Edward: Shhh! Do not disturb her sweet slumber.

William: *(Frightened)* Ned, dear soul, come to your senses. Get you up off the floor: That's all you have to do.

Edward: Angels guard thee. And you, my darling child.

William: He's near gone from us. I must venture for assistance. *(He hurries out)*

Edward: *(Looks about)* All is quiet?

A Figure *darts in and out of the shadows, ratlike:* McGinty. *He clutches the deeds to the cottage, gloatingly, and he is gone.*

He has thought all along to outwit me. That I should leave leave you homeless, my beloved! I kiss these hands that were once mine. And yours, my child. And one last time let me kiss her lips while she sleeps, for awake she would spurn me did she know it ... Yes, all's quiet now. *(He produces a phial)* It's a sin to steal – liquor. Is't sin to purloin lasting sleep with the universal antidote that – *quenches* – earthly cares?

He is about to drink the poison: Rencelaw *rushes in – followed by William – and with a deft flick of his cane sends the phial flying out of* Edward*'s hand.*

Edward: God!

Rencelaw: Nay! Take not your life, mend it!

Man: *(Without)* This way, Officer! In here, Officer!

Man, Policeman*, followed by* Floozies *and* Loafers *are arriving..*

There he is!

Policeman: *(Pushes* Rencelaw *aside)* Step aside, Jimbo!

Man: Arrest him!

Rencelaw: *(To himself; offended)* Jimbo?

All speaking together:

Policeman: Now who have we here? – *(And repeats)*

Loafer 1: What's happening, what's happening? – *(And repeats)*

Floozie 2: It's Lord Teddy, he's raving – *(And repeats)*

Floozie 3: Let me see, let me see – *(And repeats)*

Loafer 2: Sod's in the jigs – *(And repeats)*

Floozie 1: He's dying, he's dying –

Rencelaw: Jimbo? Jimbo?

Edward: *(Shivering; and a continuous gabbling mantra)* Give me a drink, give me a drink, give me a ...

William: Do something, someone. Help him, help him –

Rencelaw: Silence! ... Do you not know who I am?

William: *(Whispers to* Policeman*)* Sir Arden Rencelaw.

And the whisper – 'Sir Arden Rencelaw' – goes round, all are impressed and they pull back to watch.

Rencelaw: I have come not to judge or condemn you.

Edward: Give me a drink, give me a drink ...

Rencelaw: Consider ere it's too late.

Edward: 'Tis too late to consider – give me a drink ...

Rencelaw: You are a man and, if a man, a brother.

Edward: Give me a drink – I cannot be brother to anyone.

Rencelaw: Why?

Edward: I am lost, of no use, you put your friendship to waste here!

Rencelaw: Are you indeed lost?

Edward: Give me a drink –

Rencelaw: Are you indeed a fallen man? –

Edward: Brandy – a glass, a drop, a sip, a taste –

Rencelaw: Edward?!

Edward: I am a drunkard.

Rencelaw: ... Then you have greater claim upon my compassion.

And he produces a glass of drink – as only he can – and places it on the floor.

There is the mouthful you crave. Take it. Take it. Or stand on your feet and once more become a blessing to yourself and to those dear ones you love.

Edward: *(Shakes his head. He is becoming tearful)* That picture is too bright.

Rencelaw: You mistake, you misjudge the picture.

Edward: *(Whispers/silently)* No.

Rencelaw: Well, you now have a choice.

Edward: There is no choice. *(He's crying; hand and arm shaking, reaching, weakly, as for someone to give him the glass)*

Rencelaw: Then CRAWL!

Edward: *(Weeping; starts to crawl; stops)* It's too late.

Rencelaw: Never! You see before you one who, for twenty years, was prey to that dreadful absurdity. Come, give me your hand. Reject not my plea. The journey back, as with the journey there, begins with one step. Come, my son, my brother, enrol your name among the free, become once more an ornament to society. Be a man again.

Edward *is very weak and frail but he manages to stand. He takes* Rencelaw' *s hand and they leave together.*

William: He that lifts a fallen fellow creature be greater than the hero that conquers the world. *(Exits)*

Floozie 1: (*To heaven.*) Please, your great Majesty up there, be nice to our Lord Teddy.

And she knocks back the glass of drink that has been left on the floor.

Scene Six

Drop scene. Day. McGinty *alternates with* Rencelaw, *coming forward and retiring. An air of urgency.*

McGinty: Good news. Young Edward Kilcullen is dying.

Rencelaw: His waste in health exceeds what I'd supposed: endeavour does not prosper.

McGinty: And good news more has just arrived: my brother the master forger has expired.

Rencelaw: The special fillip must be found to rally him.

Agnes: *(Entering)* Sir! –

Rencelaw: Miss Agnes! *(Joining her, and they confer)*

McGinty: Now my brother's dead at last, I must hasten to the village, retrieve the real will from its hiding place and destroy it –

Rencelaw: You saw the lawyer at the dead of night? –

Agnes: Stealthily, Sir, put a document in a box and …

McGinty: *(With deeds to the cottage)* Then, with this, take possession of the cottage, thus concluding triumphantly my life's undertaking. *(He hurries off)*

Rencelaw: The will – ha, ha, ha! This explains Young Kilcullen's disinheritance. We have not a moment to lose. *(Calls:)* William!

William: Sir Arden!

Rencelaw: Instruct my footman run at once to Mrs Kilcullen's lodgings and tell her to prepare for a journey!

William: *(Hastening off)* Sir Arden! –

Rencelaw: And William! –

William: Sir Arden! –

Rencelaw: Race you then to Collopy's Cross, bid the postillion to halt the post-chaise and await my further orders! –

William: Sir Arden! *(And he is gone)*

Rencelaw: Miss Agnes!

Agnes: Sir! –

Rencelaw: Attend to your valise and see that my portmanteau's packed at once! –

Agnes: Sir! *(She runs)*

Rencelaw: And Miss Agnes!

Agnes: Sir! *(Stops)*

Rencelaw: Make haste!

Agnes: Sir! *(She runs)*

Rencelaw: Agnes!

Agnes: Sir!

Rencelaw: I long to hear my first name issue from her lips!

Agnes: Sir?

Rencelaw: We shall together, my dear, make the journey into night lighter-hearted with our favourite hymns. *(She races off)* Her devotion actively stirs me. But now, with God's speed, to see if we can outgo the crooked lawyer to the village and set a trap there. And if my plan succeed, might I return with the special fillip to muster a dying man? *(Hurries out)*

Scene Seven

Galloping horses: the coach is arriving, off. Night.

A landscape with moss-covered wall. Farmer *(Tom Moggan), paralytic (as in Act 1, Scene 5), is going homeward with a lantern. He thinks he hears something, then, a belch:*

Farmer: Aye! *(And is going on)*

But William *enters. He, too, has a lantern. He is bemused*

William: Tom. *('Goodnight')*

Farmer: Aye!

Now, Rencelaw *and* Agnes, *in travelling clothes. They are excited. And they have a lantern.*

Rencelaw: Cover those lanterns with your bodies! We have beaten him to it but he is on the upper road. Are you sure, Miss Agnes, this is the place?

Agnes: Brake, fern, cypress dell – Moss-covered wall! Yes!

Rencelaw: The exact spot!

Agnes: Here! No, there! No! ... I was hidden over here…

William: Grand night, Tom! *(Bemused; scratching his head)*

Farmer: Aye!

Agnes: Here!

Rencelaw: Dig! – Make haste! – *(Going out urgently, to check on* McGinty*'s approach)*

Agnes*, digging, on her hands and knees.*

Agnes: No! Here!

She has discovered that she is digging in the wrong spot and she tries another.

Rencelaw: *(Entering, briefly)* Haste, hasten or we are done for! He approaches! *(Exit)*

She hurries to dig in another spot.

Farmer: Something's afoot maybe.

William: Mary and Joseph, Tom! this be like Mother Reilly's addled eggs one time: can't make chickens or ducks of them.

Rencelaw: *(*Entering*)* What luck, Miss Agnes? He's nearly upon us!

Agnes: Here! *(And she digs a third spot)*

William: This don't tot, Sir Arden: why, she's more nuttier now than the hazel beyond!

Rencelaw: She's as sane as myself, honest William – *(And exits)*

Agnes: *(finds the tin box, opens it and produces the real will from it, and calls:)* Arden!

Rencelaw: *(Rushing in)* Agnes! *(He looks at the will)* It confirms possession of everything to Young Kilcullen. Replace the empty tin! He is here! Everyone draw back! And you, Sir, *(*Farmer*)* fetch a policeman here at once!

Farmer: Aye!

All move off. Music. And McGinty *enters, cautiously, with a lantern.*

McGinty: ... Safe. No one's about. Now to destroy the real will ...What's this? The earth looks freshly turned. I like this not ...Still, here's the box ...Empty! The will! –

Agnes: *(without)* Ha, ha, ha!

McGinty: The mad wench Agnes Earley!

Agnes: *(Entering)* Gone, gone, the bird is flown, the rightful heir shall have his own!

McGinty: *(Cane raised to beat her)* You shall pay dearly for this!

But a Policeman *rushes in, followed by* Rencelaw, William, *and* Farmer. Policeman *is pointing a pistol at* McGinty*'s head,* William *has seized his arm and* Rencelaw *holds up the will. Picture – Pause*

Rencelaw: You are trapped, Sir!

William: All day to you, Squire!

Rencelaw: *(Deftly drawing the deeds from* McGinty*'s pocket)* And as for this – the deeds to the cottage – this 'forgery' is not worth the rosin dust off a fiddler's bow to you, Sir!

McGinty: Prove it's a forgery!

Rencelaw: I see here that this document is signed by Mr Edward Kilcullen and by – Hah! Call Mr Kilcullen's wife.

William: Mrs Kilcullen!

Arabella, *bewildered, and* Alanna *enter. Cheap travelling attire.*

Rencelaw: Madam, who are you?

Arabella: Sir?

Rencelaw: State your title and your name

Arabella: Why, Mrs Kilcullen.

Rencelaw: Mrs WHAT Kilcullen?

Arabella: Mrs Arabella Kilcullen, Sir.

Rencelaw: Hah! And here is writ: PRUDENCE!

Agnes: Hah!

William: Now for you, Mr Honey!

Farmer: Aye!

Rencelaw: *(A stroke of his pen on the document before giving it to* Arabella*)* To you and your heirs, freehold and in perpetuity, is given possession of that calm retreat.

William: Take him away before I have his skin for –

Rencelaw: Nay, William – Hold, Officer! He is foul and shameful. Revenge and avarice have been his master passions and he is the perpetrator of deeds heinous: but let the superior power that has defeated him now look in Compassion's box for what might be found for this pitiable creature, who is, still, afterall, a human being. Most unfortunate man –

McGinty: Spare me. *(Darkly, to himself)*

Rencelaw: I shall see what can be done. Most unfortunate man, the deeds you have committed –

McGinty: Spare me –

Rencelaw: I shall see, Sir, what measure can be found for you!

McGinty: Spare me your speeches!

Rencelaw: What's this?

McGinty: Spare me your compassion's box!

Rencelaw: Unhappy wretch! –

McGinty: Happy wretch!

Rencelaw: Evil wretch! –

McGinty: Ha, ha, ha!

Rencelaw: Repentance is available to you!

McGinty: Who makes it available?

Rencelaw: The honest rule of the Establishment that I here represent: Church and State.

McGinty: *(To himself)* Church and State. Sir, give me the salt mines, Siberia, Van Diemen's Land. I promote life in a dungeon, in the company of foul-mouthed criminals, with the lash daily across my back, with verminous rats making dinner of my toes, than subscribe, submit or bow ever again to the scourge of your respectability.

Policeman *leads him away.*

Rencelaw: Poor, poor man. But I must follow at once and show this evidence *(the will)* to the magistrate, thence to see it safely lodged in Probate, and thence to Young Kilcullen to ascertain what effect on a dying man the knowledge that he is now a wealthy one.

William: What blessings, at all, at all, can repay you, Sir?

Rencelaw: My own approving conscience, honest William. *(He goes to* Agnes*)*

Agnes: Arden, you're exhausted.

Rencelaw: *(Has to agree that he is)* And with heavy heart I leave you.

Agnes: God grant you will return, sometime, with lighter one and refreshed.

He leaves.

William: The heart of a feeling man, Tom Moggan, be like a tree that's wounded yet still gives forth its precious sap.

Farmer: Aye! Children and chickens must always be a-pickin'. *(Closing in, with his boot, one of the holes dug by* Agnes*)*

Scene Eight

Interior of the cottage. A pretty picture. Arabella *and* Alanna *are completing a tapestry, a symmetry of motion between mother and daughter. They sing, unself-consciously, as they work, a duet:*

Soft, soft music is stealing,
Sweet, sweet lingers the strain,
Loud, loud, now it is pealing,
Waking the echoes again ...
Yes, yes, yes, yes
Waking the echoes again.

Join, join children of sadness,
Send, send sorrow away,
Now, now changing to gladness,
Warble a beautiful lay ...
Yes, yes, yes, yes,
Warble a beautiful lay.

Without, a cheer from the Villagers

Alanna: What can that be, Mother?

Arabella: I know not, my dear.

Edward: *(without)* Thank you, thank you, kind friends and neighbours!

Alanna: It sounds like ...

Arabella: Edward!

Alanna: Father!

Edward: Where is my dear, my beloved wife? *(Entering, well-dressed)*

Arabella: Edward! Is it you?

Edward: It is I! My blessed one!

Arabella: Oh my dear, dear, dear, dear husband! *(As they embrace)*

Edward: And my child, my child!

Alanna: Father! Father!

Arabella: Bounteous heaven! *(To heaven)*

Alanna: Accept our thanks! *(To heaven)*

Arabella: Oh my beloved, are you returned to me?

Edward: *(Another embrace)* And wiser. *(He is in tears)*

Alanna: He is crying, Mother. Mother, you are crying too!

Edward: Yes, my child, we weep. But these are different tears to those we have known.

Arabella: Tears of joy. And our past troubles now are as nothing compared to this happiness.

A cheer from without.

Villagers: Hooray for Sir Arden Rencelaw!

Rencelaw *comes in, followed by* William *and others.*

Arabella: Sir, what words can express our gratitude?

Rencelaw: Pay thanks where it is due. *(i.e. to heaven)* I am rewarded in your happiness.

Alanna *presents him with a little bunch of flowers.*

Dear child.

Edward: I shall not wrong your selfless nature, Sir Arden, by fulsome show of praise, but humbly beg that heaven gives me the strength to continue in the path adorned by your example.

Rencelaw: (*Epilogue)* What joy can equal the sensations of a thinking being returned from futility? With what happiness the erstwhile prisoned heart beats in the rediscovery of life's beauty. How it pulses with the spirit of the earth! And the soul listens to its own music – the diminuendo that held on – now swell in tune with the Infinite, the great mystery we all share.

Now Full Company. *They pair as appropriate. And, led by* Edward, *they sing:*

> There came a change – the clouds rolled off,
> A light fell on my brain,
> And, like the passing of a dream,
> That cometh not again,
> The darkness of my spirit fled,
> I saw the gulf before,
> I shuddered at the waste behind,
> And am a man once more

And – Tableau.

Carysfort Press was formed in the summer of 1998. It receives annual funding from the Arts Council.

The directors believe that drama is playing an ever-increasing role in today's society and that enjoyment of the theatre, both professional and amateur, currently plays a central part in Irish culture.

The Press aims to produce high quality publications which, though written and/or edited by academics, will be made accessible to a general readership. The organisation would also like to provide a forum for critical thinking in the Arts in Ireland, again keeping the needs and interests of the general public in view.

The company publishes contemporary Irish writing for and about the theatre.

Editorial and publishing inquiries to:

CARYSFORT PRESS Ltd

58 Woodfield, Scholarstown Road,
Rathfarnham, Dublin 16,
Republic of Ireland

T (353 1) 493 7383 F (353 1) 406 9815
e: info@carysfortpress.com

www.carysfortpress.com

NEW TITLES

GOETHE AND SCHUBERT

ACROSS THE DIVIDE
EDITED BY LORRAINE BYRNE & DAN FARRELLY

Proceedings of the International Conference, 'Goethe and Schubert in Perspective and Performance', Trinity College Dublin, 2003. This volume includes essays by leading scholars – Barkhoff, Boyle, Byrne, Canisius, Dürr, Fischer, Hill, Kramer, Lamport, Lund, Meikle, Newbould, Norman McKay, White, Whitton, Wright, Youens – on Goethe's musicality and his relationship to Schubert; Schubert's contribution to sacred music and the Lied and his setting of Goethe's Singspiel, Claudine. A companion volume of this Singspiel (with piano reduction and English translation) is also available.

ISBN 1-904505-04-X
Goethe and Schubert: Across the Divide. €25

ISBN 0-9544290-0-1
Goethe and Schubert: 'Claudine von Villa Bella'. €14

PLAYBOYS OF THE WESTERN WORLD

PRODUCTION HISTORIES
EDITED BY ADRIAN FRAZIER

'Playboys of the Western World is a model of contemporary performance studies.'

'The book is remarkably well-focused: half is a series of production histories of Playboy performances through the twentieth century in the UK, Northern Ireland, the USA, and Ireland. The remainder focuses on one contemporary performance, that of Druid Theatre, as directed by Garry Hynes. The various contemporary social issues that are addressed in relation to Synge's play and this performance of it give the volume an additional interest: it shows how the arts matter.' – Kevin Barry

ISBN 1-904505-06-6
€20

CRITICAL MOMENTS

FINTAN O'TOOLE ON MODERN IRISH THEATRE EDITED BY JULIA FURAY & REDMOND O'HANLON

This new book on the work of Fintan O'Toole, the internationally acclaimed theatre critic and cultural commentator, offers percussive analyses and assessments of the major plays and playwrights in the canon of modern Irish theatre. Fearless and provocative in his judgements, O'Toole is essential reading for anyone interested in criticism or in the current state of Irish theatre.

ISBN 1-904505-03-1
€20

THE POWER OF LAUGHTER

EDITED BY ERIC WEITZ

The collection draws on a wide range of perspectives and voices including critics, playwrights, directors and performers. The result is a series of fascinating and provocative debates about the myriad functions of comedy in contemporary Irish theatre. Anna McMullan

As Stan Laurel said, it takes only an onion to cry. Peel it and weep. Comedy is harder. These essays listen to the power of laughter. They hear the tough heart of Irish theatre – hard and wicked and funny. Frank McGuinness

ISBN 1-904505-05-8
€20

GEORG BÜCHNER: WOYZECK

A NEW TRANSLATION BY DAN FARRELLY

The most up-to-date German scholarship of Thomas Michael Mayer and Burghard Dedner has finally made it possible to establish an authentic sequence of scenes. The wide-spread view that this play is a prime example of loose, open theatre is no longer sustainable. Directors and teachers are challenged to "read it again".

ISBN 1-904505-02-3
€10

SACRED PLAY

SOUL JOURNEYS IN CONTEMPORARY IRISH THEATRE BY ANNE F. O'REILLY

'Theatre as a space or container for sacred play allows audiences to glimpse mystery and to experience transformation. This book charts how Irish playwrights negotiate the labyrinth of the Irish soul and shows how their plays contribute to a poetics of Irish culture that enables a new imagining. Playwrights discussed are: McGuinness, Murphy, Friel, Le Marquand Hartigan, Burke Brogan, Harding, Meehan, Carr, Parker, Devlin, and Barry.'

ISBN 1-904505-07-4
€25

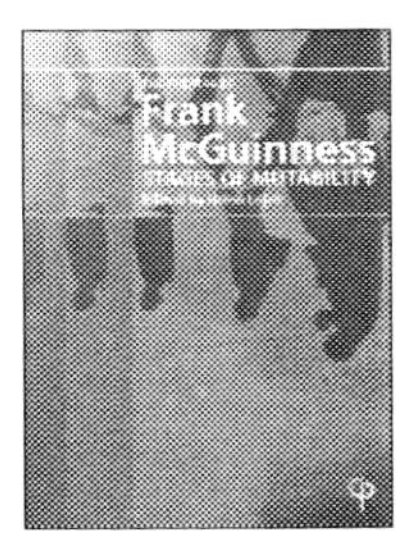

THE THEATRE OF FRANK MCGUINNESS

STAGES OF MUTABILITY
EDITED BY HELEN LOJEK

The first edited collection of essays about internationally renowned Irish playwright Frank McGuinness focuses on both performance and text. Interpreters come to diverse conclusions, creating a vigorous dialogue that enriches understanding and reflects a strong consensus about the value of McGuinness's complex work.

ISBN 1-904505-01-5
€20

THE THEATRE OF MARINA CARR

"BEFORE RULES WAS MADE" - EDITED BY ANNA MCMULLAN & CATHY LEENEY

As the first published collection of articles on the theatre of Marina Carr, this volume explores the world of Carr's theatrical imagination, the place of her plays in contemporary theatre in Ireland and abroad and the significance of her highly individual voice.

ISBN 0-9534-2577-0
€20

THEATRE OF SOUND

RADIO AND THE DRAMATIC IMAGINATION
BY DERMOT RATTIGAN

An innovative study of the challenges that radio drama poses to the creative imagination of the writer, the production team, and the listener.

"A remarkably fine study of radio drama – everywhere informed by the writer's professional experience of such drama in the making…A new theoretical and analytical approach – informative, illuminating and at all times readable." *Richard Allen Cave*

ISBN 0-9534-2575-4
€20

HAMLET

THE SHAKESPEAREAN DIRECTOR
BY MIKE WILCOCK

"This study of the Shakespearean director as viewed through various interpretations of HAMLET is a welcome addition to our understanding of how essential it is for a director to have a clear vision of a great play. It is an important study from which all of us who love Shakespeare and who understand the importance of continuing contemporary exploration may gain new insights."

From the Foreword, by Joe Dowling, Artistic Director, The Guthrie Theater, Minneapolis, MN

ISBN 1-904505-00-7
€20

TALKING ABOUT TOM MURPHY

EDITED BY NICHOLAS GRENE

Talking About Tom Murphy is shaped around the six plays in the landmark Abbey Theatre Murphy Season of 2001, assembling some of the best-known commentators on his work: Fintan O'Toole, Chris Morash, Lionel Pilkington, Alexandra Poulain, Shaun Richards, Nicholas Grene and Declan Kiberd.

ISBN 0-9534-2579-7
€15

THE IRISH HARP BOOK

BY SHEILA LARCHET CUTHBERT

This is a facsimile of the edition originally published by Mercier Press in 1993. There is a new preface by Sheila Larchet Cuthbert, and the biographical material has been updated. It is a collection of studies and exercises for the use of teachers and pupils of the Irish harp.

ISBN 1-904505-08-2
€40

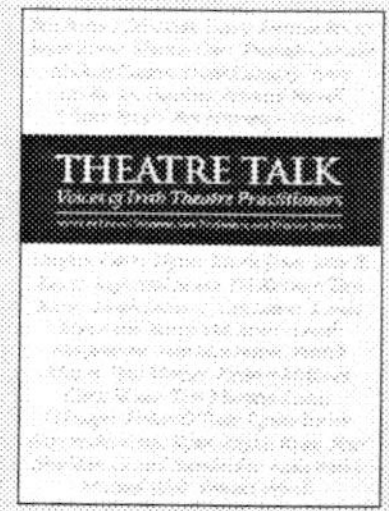

THEATRE TALK

VOICES OF IRISH THEATRE PRACTITIONERS
EDITED BY LILIAN CHAMBERS &
GER FITZGIBBON

"This book is the right approach - asking practitioners what they feel."
Sebastian Barry, Playwright

"... an invaluable and informative collection of interviews with those who make and shape the landscape of Irish Theatre."
Ben Barnes, Artistic Director of the Abbey Theatre

ISBN 0-9534-2576-2
€20